KRISTEN PARKER

When Fates Drown in Silence

Contents

One

The Last Note of the Weavers

Ash fell like snow over the ruins of Ilyndor.

The once-great city—center of the Weave, seat of the Fate-Wrought Choirs—was now nothing more than cracked marble bones and hollow echoes. The great domes of the Hall of Threads lay shattered, spider-webbed under the weight of time and war. Aris Caelen walked beneath them in silence, boots sinking into soot and crushed songglass, the air thick with memory and ruin.

His cloak dragged behind him like a funeral banner. Wind snaked through broken arches, stirring the lingering whispers of a melody no one dared to sing.

He shouldn't have returned.

But the pull had grown stronger these past nights. A tug at the back of his mind. Not pain. Not warning. A resonance. Like a chord he once knew, now buried under the silence that ruled this place.

Aris paused in the central chamber—the Weaving Floor. Runes once etched in gold now glowed faintly beneath centuries of dust. Twelve looms had stood here once, circled around the Anchorstone. Twelve weavers, twelve voices, twelve threads sung into fate each dawn. Now, only silence answered.

Until—

A hum.

Low. Subtle. Barely there.

He turned slowly.

One loom—half buried beneath collapsed beams and rusted chains—pulsed faintly. A heartbeat. A flicker of light from within its ruined core. His own pulse stuttered.

No loom should hum. Not anymore.

Aris stepped closer, careful not to disturb the fragile balance of stone and bone. The hum grew louder—not sound, but vibration. It moved through his skin, into his teeth, deep into the threadlines of his blood.

And then he saw it.

Beneath the cracked ironwood frame, among the wreckage, nestled in the remains of forgotten threads—

A single strand. Glowing. Intact.

Gold, yes. But shot through with silver and violet.

Living thread.

Impossible.

His knees hit the floor before he realized he'd dropped. His hands hovered above it, reverent. It shimmered with the last echoes of its song, barely surviving—but alive. As he reached out, the hum sharpened.

Then—

Words.

Soft. In a voice he hadn't heard in years. A voice that should have been dead.

"Aris."

He froze.

"Aris, do you remember?"

The thread pulsed. A flare of memory struck him like lightning—

A girl.

Silver-braided hair.
  Eyes like dusk.

A voice that bent fate.

Lyra.

The air cracked. The silence fought back.

The humming thread lashed out, a flare of light erupting from the loom as if it had waited too long to be found. Aris was thrown back, hit the marble floor with a grunt.

The thread snapped loose—

—and wrapped around his wrist.

He gasped. His veins lit with gold.

The silence screamed.

And deep in the broken city, something else stirred.

Not just memory.

Not just fate.

The Void had seen the spark.

And it was listening.

The glow from the thread faded slowly, retreating beneath his skin as if afraid of the light it had released.

Aris lay still, chest heaving, staring up at the fractured dome of the Hall. Dust floated through the shafts of dying light, golden and ash-blended, like snow falling in slow motion. The silence that followed wasn't empty.

It *watched.*

The world had rules. Threads unraveled, songs went quiet, and fate no longer spoke. That was the pact. The end of the Weave. The end of *her.* No one had touched a living thread in ten years, not since the Silence took the sky.

But now—

Now the thread pulsed faintly beneath his skin, coiled like a serpent around his forearm, woven into his very blood.

"Lyra," he whispered aloud.

The name seared the air.

He hadn't said it in years.

Not since the War of Splinters. Not since the voice that could bend the tapestry of time itself had vanished in a blaze of fatefire. He had buried her name, sealed it behind guilt and broken oaths.

But the thread remembered.

The thread had *always* remembered.

Aris pushed himself upright, shaking, sweat streaking his face despite the cool air. His fingers hovered over the point where the thread entered his wrist. It didn't hurt. It *sang*—quietly, insistently, like it was calling to its origin.

He looked around the hall.

"What did you do, Lyra?" he asked the shadows.

The answer was silence.

But the wind shifted.

He stood, pacing backward, mind racing. The Void wouldn't ignore this. If the thread was alive, then *fate* was alive—and if fate was alive, the Unraveling had failed. Or worse... it had only paused.

He needed to leave.

Now.

The ruins of Ilyndor were buried deep in the mountains, beyond the reach of most. But there were things that wandered the dead halls. Beings that once served the Weavers and now served nothing but entropy. The Silence had left them hungry.

And the hum of the thread was a beacon.

He swept his cloak around his shoulder, eyes locking on the distant archway that led back toward the hollow roads. He would need to pass through the Threadspire graveyards, and that would be dangerous enough without—

A whisper. Soft.

Close.

"Aris..."

He spun, dagger in hand, heart hammering.

No one.

Just the broken loom behind him.

But the voice...

It wasn't imagined. It was real. It had shape. It had memory.

He walked slowly back to the loom. The glow was fading now, the last pulse of light dimming into stillness.

He knelt and traced the edge of the wood, now split and charred. As his fingers brushed the center groove—the heart of the loom—he felt a pulse.

Not his.

Hers.

A final imprint.

Lyra had used this loom. Not just touched it. *Woven* into it. But when? How? She had never been allowed here, never trained in the deep halls. She was—

His breath caught.

She was always *more* than they understood. More than the Choir allowed. Her voice hadn't simply woven fate.

It *rewrote* it.

And that's why the Order had feared her.

That's why Aris had been commanded to stop her.

That's why she was dead.

Or should have been.

He rose, jaw set.

He needed answers.

If this thread existed, others might. And if Lyra's essence was woven into it, there was a chance—gods help him—a chance she was still *out there.*

Alive.

Changed.

Forgotten.

He looked toward the northern arch. Toward the Hollow Vale. Toward the old songs buried in the dust of stars and broken timelines.

He took one last look at the loom.

And turned.

Behind him, in the shadows of the hall, something moved.

A flicker of robes.

A whisper of thread.

And then—

Silence.

But Aris didn't look back.

He already knew what he'd find if he did.

The Void had seen the light.

And now it was coming.

Two

The Girl with the Stolen Voice

The first thing she remembered was light.

Not bright.

Not pure.

It was a fractured sort of light, like sunlight filtered through broken glass—scattered, trembling, uncertain. It touched her skin in pieces, painting her arms with shifting warmth as if deciding whether she belonged to the living.

Lyra opened her eyes to a canopy of gold-veined leaves.

The trees above her swayed with a soundless rhythm, branches curving like fingers casting spells overhead. The sky beyond them was pale and shivering, its blue faded to the color of lost parchment. She blinked slowly, one breath—then another. The air smelled of ironroot and ash-mint, the kind of blend that only grew in glades no one named.

Where was she?

She sat up too fast.

Pain lanced through her skull—sharp and blinding, followed by a hollow ache behind her eyes. She gasped but no sound came. Her lips parted. She tried again.

Nothing.

No voice.

No whisper.

No breath of a word.

The glade fell heavy around her in response. As if the trees themselves mourned the silence that clung to her throat like a chain. She pressed a trembling hand to her chest, then her neck. Her pulse was steady, but *wrong*, like it beat to a rhythm that didn't belong to her.

Something was missing.

She didn't know what.

Or *who*.

Her eyes scanned the clearing.

It was a wide glade, ringed by roots that curled like old stone carvings. The ground was soft and overgrown with silvergrass and pale moss, and in the very center was a pool— clear, motionless, and perfectly round. Its surface did not ripple. No wind touched it.

And yet it *hummed*.

Not loudly.

Not even audibly.

But she felt it. A vibration beneath her skin. A distant melody brushing her bones.

She rose, limbs stiff but not broken, barefoot and aching. Her dress—simple linen, once white—was scorched at the hem. She reached for the nearest tree to steady herself, and the bark crumbled beneath her fingers like charred paper.

She recoiled.

A whisper slid through the leaves.

Not a sound.

A shape.

"Lyra."

Her breath caught.

Her name. Someone had spoken it. But it hadn't come from around her.

It had come from *inside* the wind.

She turned slowly, eyes wide.

"Lyra."

Again.

More insistent.

She stumbled toward the pool, her feet making no sound. The air thickened as she approached, growing heavier with each step until it felt like she was walking through a memory made solid.

The pool glowed faintly now. Silver light, deep and soft.

She knelt beside it, leaned forward.

Her reflection stared back at her—but her eyes were wrong.

They glowed.

Faintly violet. Threaded with gold.

Not normal.

Not human.

She touched her face and the reflection rippled. In its place appeared a flash—an image not her own:

A great hall in ruin.

A loom burning.

A man standing in shadow, blood on his hands.

And a name on his lips.

Not hers.

But one she *should* know.

The vision shattered.

The pool went still.

She tried to scream, but the silence in her throat only deepened. Her heart pounded. She clutched at her chest, a terrible ache spreading from beneath her ribs.

And then—

Music.

Soft. Distant.

A melody with no words.

Not played on instrument or sung.

But woven.

It came from the trees now, threading through branches like wind-chimes made from memory. It curled around her ears and she *knew*—

It was *hers.*

Her song.

Forgotten. Stolen. Broken apart and scattered.

But not lost.

Not yet.

The trees leaned closer, groaning under the weight of unseen things. Their leaves shimmered with runes she didn't recognize but somehow *understood.* Threads of language wrapped in silence, coiling through the air as if urging her forward.

She stood again.

This time stronger.

And followed the music.

The glade narrowed into a path carved by footfalls she couldn't remember making. Each step drew her deeper into the woods. Shadows swirled and fled at her approach. Her fingers brushed against bark and stone, and her magic—though sealed—responded with flinching flickers.

The silence that had imprisoned her voice wasn't natural.

It was *inflicted.*

She had been silenced.

Not by injury.

By *spell.*

And spells could be broken.

The melody grew louder.

Not in sound—but presence. It pressed against her senses like a heartbeat just behind a wall. It tugged at her, and she let it. She walked for what felt like hours, until the forest broke into another clearing—smaller, stranger.

There, standing in the center, was a tree made of glass.

Its trunk shimmered with threads of silver light. Its roots pulsed through the earth like veins. And suspended from its crystalline branches were dozens—*hundreds*—of small glowing objects.

Not fruit.

Not stars.

Names.

Spoken names, preserved in light, hanging like lanterns.

Lyra stepped forward, breath stolen once more, but not from silence.

From awe.

The tree *remembered.*

Each name shimmered with memory. Each glowed with power. Each sang a single note in a vast, unfinished symphony. But none of them were hers.

She searched anyway.

Her hands trembled as she reached up, brushing the edge of one glowing sigil. The moment she did, a rush of feeling surged through her—a moment of someone else's life, of love lost, a final breath before a thread snapped.

She staggered back.

The song faltered.

And then—

The wind changed.

No longer warm.

It hissed.

"She wakes."

The words slithered through the trees like smoke.

The melody shattered.

The silence grew sharp.

Cold crept in.

The forest held its breath.

Something had *seen* her.

Something that *hated* noise.

Lyra turned, heart racing.

Shapes stirred beyond the clearing—shadows that moved wrong, stretching and breaking and reforming with each breath. Their eyes glowed faint white. Their mouths didn't open.

But their presence screamed.

Voidborn.

Servants of the Silence.

Drawn to what should not be remembered.

Lyra ran.

Her bare feet pounded across root and rock. The forest blurred around her. The melody returned—not behind her, but *within* her. It surged from her chest, silent but strong, like thunder under skin.

She couldn't scream.

But the *song* could.

Light flared from her fingers.

Threadlines—faint and broken—snapped into the air around her.

The Voidborn recoiled, hissed, dissolved into mist.

Lyra stumbled forward, the last of her strength leaving her.

And then—

Arms caught her.

Firm.

Steady.

A voice, low and strange and *familiar*:

"You shouldn't be awake."

She looked up.

Saw eyes like broken skies.

Eyes that once held her name.

He didn't recognize her.

Not yet.

But she remembered.

Not everything.

Just enough.

Just *him*.

And as darkness pulled her under again, the melody wrapped around her—

A thread beginning to sing once more.

She drifted on the edge of consciousness, not quite asleep, not yet awake. The melody lingered — no longer a haunting fragment but a fuller shape, looping in the space behind her ribs. It pulsed like a second heartbeat. It was warm, and it hurt.

When Lyra woke again, it was to candlelight and shadows.

She lay wrapped in blankets woven from starcloth — that

fine, shimmer-threaded material that no one had made in a decade. The scent of yarrow root and smoked pine filled her lungs. Her throat burned with thirst and silence, but her hands no longer trembled.

She blinked against the soft golden light.

A fire cracked nearby.

And a figure sat in its glow, sharpening a blade against his boot.

He hadn't heard her stir.

She knew his silhouette. The broad shoulders. The tense line of his spine. The way his hands moved, too precisely, like he didn't trust his own strength.

She knew him, but not *why*.

He turned slightly.

And Lyra's breath caught.

He was older than she remembered — if her memory could be trusted. His hair was darker, longer, streaked with threads of silver like lightning caught in obsidian. A scar ran from his temple to the hinge of his jaw. His clothes were layered, worn, but his hands were still steady. And his eyes—

Storm-grey. Wild with thought. Familiar in the deepest way.

He glanced toward her now, sensing movement.

Their eyes met.

His lips parted — not in recognition, but in caution.

"You're awake," he said softly, voice low and rough from disuse.

She nodded.

Her hand flew to her throat.

Nothing.

Still mute.

She tried to sit up, and he was at her side in an instant, one hand outstretched.

"Easy," he said. "Your system's still rebalancing. The magic in the glade… it's older than anything I've seen."

She froze.

Did he know what she was? Who she had been?

He hesitated.

"I'm Aris," he said.

Her heart stuttered.

Yes.

She *knew.*

But there was no flicker of recognition in his face. No pain. No regret. Just a stranger's kindness cloaked in war-worn fatigue.

He continued, settling beside her as the fire popped. "I found you in the Threadwood. Near the Glass Tree."

Her eyes widened.

He nodded. "Didn't think anyone made it out of that place alive, let alone intact."

She tried again to speak. Her mouth moved. No sound.

He watched her carefully.

"You're not cursed," he said, as if anticipating her fear. "Not in the traditional sense. It's more like… your thread was sealed. Your voice — your magic — folded inward."

She tilted her head.

"How do I know that?" he echoed the question she couldn't ask. "Because I used to be a Fate-Weaver."

Her breath stilled.

"I left the Order," he added, voice quieter now. "A long time ago."

She didn't look away.

He shifted, leaned forward, elbows on knees.

"You've got something inside you. Something humming. I felt it when I touched you. Your thread… it's unlike anything I've ever seen." He paused. "It was singing."

Her eyes flickered.

He nodded again. "I thought that kind of song was lost. Or… taken."

She wanted to scream his name. To throw the truth at him. *You silenced me.*

But her voice was still locked behind magic, and the man before her wasn't the same one who had stood in the ruin of the Hall with blood on his hands and her name on his lips.

He hadn't remembered.

And somehow, that hurt more than if he had.

Aris glanced over at her, then reached for something beside the fire — a silver pendant.

It was hers.

Delicate. Woven from fine song-thread and shaped like a falling star.

"I found this in your grip," he said. "You were clutching it like it was the last thing you remembered."

He held it out to her.

She took it carefully, fingers brushing his.

Another spark.

Another flash:

Rain. A violin. His mouth on hers beneath a sky unraveling.

It was gone in an instant.

She flinched.

So did he.

"What was that?" he whispered.

She shook her head.

"I've seen echoes before," he murmured, more to himself.

"But that… felt like a memory."

She touched the pendant to her chest.

And the silence in her throat… *shifted.*

A crack in the dam.

A tremor in the seal.

She gasped.

Aris was beside her in a second. "Are you alright?"

She looked at him, trembling, and for the first time managed a whisper — not spoken, not heard — but shaped in magic.

A name.

His.

Aris blinked.

The fire flickered.

He turned slowly to stare at her, face pale.

"What did you just say?" he asked.

She didn't answer.

Couldn't.

But the pendant flared in her hand.

And Aris stood like he'd been struck.

"That's not possible," he said.

But he already knew.

He stepped back, the truth beginning to splinter through memory he'd sealed long ago.

She tried to reach for him.

He backed away.

His eyes — those storm-lit eyes — were wide with something fragile and terrified.

Recognition.

Realization.

Regret.

He whispered her name.

This time aloud.

"Lyra."

And the wind, waiting just outside the cabin door, carried it like a promise into the night.

Three

When Silence Spoke

The storm rolled in as Aris crossed into the Bonehearth Pines—low clouds, not of thunder, but *weight*, heavy with unshed magic. The sky hung low, like it too was waiting to break. He pressed forward, the living thread coiled beneath the skin of his wrist pulsing faster with each step.

It wanted something.

No—*someone.*

The thread was leading him toward her, threading through wind and earth like a whisper that refused to die. But it was also humming with unease. He could feel it. A wrongness beneath the soil. A tension in the roots. Something else walked here.

Something that didn't belong.

Twilight bled into the trees, the pines towering black above him, their trunks bone-pale against the dusk. Snow hadn't fallen, but frost crept along every surface—on the rocks, the bark, even the air itself, curling white as he exhaled.

Still, he kept walking. The thread tugged him east.

He hadn't told Lyra.

Not yet.

Not about what he'd seen in her eyes when she tried to speak.

Not about the moment her pendant glowed and memory *quivered*, and a thousand buried things rose from the crypt he'd built inside himself.

Not about the terror laced into the threads of fate itself.

Because whatever power slept in her… it was waking.

And it had not come alone.

Aris stepped into a clearing ringed by stones older than the cities of men. Time pooled here. He could feel it. Thick. Slow. Beneath his boots, runes etched into the frost flickered—sigils of the Old Tongue. The Weavers' language.

He knelt beside one.

Ran a gloved hand across its surface.

The rune flared.

The forest *exhaled.*

And the silence broke.

But not into sound.

Into *presence.*

He froze.

There was no warning.

No shadow.

No footstep.

Just cold.

Sudden and absolute.

Behind him, the wind stilled.

Aris rose slowly, muscles tight, heart already thudding.

And then—

A whisper.

Not a breath. Not a voice.

A *replication.*

His name, formed in a cadence not its own.

"Aris."

He turned.

And saw nothing.

Nothing—but *absence.*

A figure stood at the edge of the clearing. Humanoid in shape. Wrapped in smoke and ash. Its outline flickered as if reality itself was unwilling to accept it.

And its face—gods, its *face*—

No eyes.

No mouth.

Just a smooth canvas of pale skin pulled too tight over bone.

But the voice came again.

"Aris."

It didn't speak.

It *stole.*

The voice belonged to Lyra.

It *used* her voice.

Aris stumbled back, bile rising in his throat.

Voidborn.

Not one of the minor remnants—no flickerling or wraith.

This was something deeper. A thing that should have never left the fractures between time. A creature born of silence itself. And it was here.

In the living world.

His dagger slid free with a hiss, etched in soulsteel, runes pulsing down the edge. It would hold. He hoped.

The creature tilted its head.

"Do you remember her?" it asked—again in Lyra's stolen

voice. "Do you remember what you did?"

Aris didn't answer.

"Did you think fate would forget?" it continued. "Did you think silence would be enough to bury her song?"

He stepped sideways, circling, eyes scanning for threads in the air.

There were none.

No fate lines.

No paths.

The creature had no thread.

It was *unwritten.*

He lunged.

Steel kissed smoke.

The creature blinked—one instant there, the next behind him.

It whispered again.

"She wakes. The song begins. And the end begins with it."

He turned, blade slashing a second time, but the creature caught it.

With a hand.

A hand of bone and mist.

The runes on his dagger flared, screaming.

The blade shattered.

The shock knocked Aris backward.

He hit the ground, shoulder burning.

The creature stepped forward.

The ground *froze* beneath its feet.

"You severed her voice," it said. "And now we will sever yours."

Aris reached into his coat, grabbed the vials hidden beneath the inner lining—each filled with Threadfire.

He threw them.

The clearing exploded.

Light.

Heat.

Burning song.

The creature screamed—a soundless rupture that split the air and sent birds fleeing for miles.

Aris rolled away, ears bleeding, vision fractured. The clearing burned blue.

The Voidborn vanished.

But its message remained, carved into the stone where it had stood:

SHE WILL SING YOU INTO ASH.

He stared at it, breath ragged.

This wasn't over.

Not even close.

The creature hadn't come for him.

It had come to warn.

To *provoke.*

To *awaken.*

Lyra's thread hadn't just survived.

It had *summoned* the silence.

And whatever came next—

He wasn't sure if he could stop it.

He only knew one thing:

If she remembered what he had done…

If she remembered the truth…

Not even fate would forgive him.

The trees whispered like dying men.

As the last of the blue fire faded from the clearing, Aris

staggered to his feet, coughing against the smoke that no longer came from burning wood, but from magic scorched too deeply into the earth to be natural. The sigils on the ancient stones had dimmed to gray ash, their power spent—or silenced.

His dagger was gone.

His left arm trembled from the impact, already darkening with bruises. A trail of blood tickled down the side of his neck from where the creature's scream had burst something inside his ear.

But none of that mattered.

What mattered was that it had *spoken in her voice*.

He gritted his teeth, clenching the broken hilt in his hand. Voidborn were supposed to be mindless. Shadows that slipped between cracks in fate, feeding off the unraveling threads left behind. Not mimics. Not *sentient*. And certainly not capable of *speech*.

And yet…

"Do you remember what you did?"

He couldn't get the words out of his head. The tone. The *exact* intonation of Lyra's voice—the way it used to sound when she stood behind him, arms crossed, teasing him after a battle narrowly won. Before her voice could bend timelines. Before the Choir had branded her dangerous. Before *he* had silenced it.

"Damn it," Aris whispered into the smoke, jaw tightening.

The wind shifted again. This time not with warning—but with *invitation*. The living thread inside his wrist pulsed once, then again—harder. It wanted movement. It wanted him to follow.

But follow *what*?

He looked down at the stone where the Voidborn had stood,

now scorched black and cracked at the edges. The phrase remained burned into it, untouched by the Threadfire:

SHE WILL SING YOU INTO ASH.

Aris bent low and touched the edge of the carving with trembling fingers. The weave recognized truth when it was spoken in magic. And this was truth. A *prophecy*, of sorts.

Or a warning.

He turned back toward the forest's edge. The sky had grown darker. Somewhere far beyond the trees, thunder grumbled— a slow, deliberate sound, as if the heavens were clearing their throat.

He needed to find Lyra.

Now.

He reached into his coat again and withdrew a small spindle—an old Weavers' relic. A personal thread tracker. It only worked if two souls had ever shared a fate-knot. Most had been destroyed during the Eclipse War, but he'd kept this one. Hidden. Buried.

For her.

He held it out. Whispered her name.

Nothing.

The spindle turned once. Twice.

Then stilled.

Then—*shuddered*.

The golden thread wrapped around his wrist *tightened* like it felt her too. It pulled sharply west. Toward the broken pass that led into the Vale of Hollows.

Toward her.

He tightened his cloak, shoved the shard of his ruined dagger into a loop on his belt, and began to run.

He moved fast, winding through trees that leaned as if trying to hear him pass. The scent of burned thread lingered on his coat. As night descended, the air grew colder—not with winter, but with *emptiness*. There were no insects. No birds. No wolves. Even the rustle of leaves had grown hesitant.

Silence had a *weight* now. And it pressed against his back with every step.

He reached the edge of the forest by midnight. Below him, the valley spread wide—a pale scar beneath a waning moon. He saw the remnants of what had once been a village. Only outlines remained. Foundations. A shattered well.

And in the center—

A woman.

Kneeling.

Hair like silver ash caught in wind.

A thread of light looping from her chest into the sky.

The thread pulsed in sync with the one on his wrist.

Lyra.

Aris nearly shouted, but caught himself. Instead, he approached in silence, wary now. The wind shifted. Something else stirred at the edge of the vale.

As he reached the base of the hill, Lyra looked up. Her eyes met his.

Wide. Bright. Alive.

And *terrified*.

She pointed behind him.

Too late.

A second Voidborn dropped from the trees, its body a blur of shadow and hunger. Aris twisted, drawing the shard of soulsteel in one hand and a spellflame in the other. The flame sputtered.

The creature hissed—not with sound, but with silence so

pure it *ate* the light.

Lyra raised both hands.

And something inside her *snapped*.

The thread from her chest flared bright.

Music—*real music*—echoed in the air.

A single, pure note.

The Voidborn froze.

So did Aris.

The note climbed, warping the air.

The creature screamed—not with Lyra's voice this time, but with its own—a high-pitched, breaking sound like mirrors exploding in reverse.

Then it burst into ash.

Silence returned.

Aris turned to Lyra, stunned.

She stared at her own hands, breathing hard, eyes wide with something between awe and terror.

He stepped forward. "Lyra—"

She didn't move.

Didn't blink.

Her lips parted.

And for the first time, her voice came back—not as a whisper.

But as a *song*.

Soft. Trembling.

One line.

One sentence.

"They are coming for us both."

Then she collapsed.

And the stars above them began to dim.

Four

The Melody Beneath the Mask

The cave was cold.

Not the kind that bit the skin or stiffened fingers, but the sort of cold that sat in the *bones*. Lyra blinked against dim lantern light. The stone walls flickered with orange shadow, their curves worn by centuries of dripping water and forgotten magic.

There were voices.

Muffled, urgent, layered one over the other like threads spun too tightly.

She pushed herself upright, spine aching, breath thin. Her throat felt raw, as though something ancient had clawed its way free of it. She remembered the valley. The creature. The song.

And Aris.

His name sent a jolt through her.

She looked around.

The space was narrow, domed, carved from rock. Stalactites hung like frozen teeth overhead. At the far side of the chamber, a black curtain stirred—entrance or exit, she couldn't tell.

The voices were behind it.

She pulled the rough blanket tighter around her shoulders and stood, legs unsteady. Beneath her bare feet, the stone was etched—circular lines, radiating from the center like the rings of a shattered loom.

A sigil of the Old Resistance.

Someone had drawn it here, reclaimed the symbol like a prayer.

She pushed aside the curtain and stepped into light.

The corridor beyond widened into a chamber thick with activity. Torches burned in sconces hammered directly into stone. Maps, constellations, and thread diagrams covered the walls. Shelves sagged under the weight of salvaged relics. At the center, a long wooden table was surrounded by figures in dark coats, hoods pushed back, weapons within reach.

They looked up as she entered.

Silence fell.

Then one stepped forward.

A woman—tall, silver hair coiled into a crown of braids, a scar slicing from her eyebrow to her temple. She wore a long threadcloak, its hem embroidered with names. Her presence filled the room.

"You're awake," she said.

Lyra nodded, cautiously.

The woman studied her.

"You sang."

It wasn't a question.

Lyra's pulse quickened.

"You held off a Voidborn with *nothing* but your voice," the woman continued, folding her arms. "That shouldn't be possible."

Lyra gestured to her throat, shook her head.

"Not anymore?" the woman guessed.

A pause.

Lyra nodded slowly.

The woman sighed.

"Well, that explains the ripple."

Another figure stepped forward, voice sharper. "Or a trap. You saw how the sky shifted. We all felt it. The Choir will have felt it too."

The others murmured agreement.

"She's a Threadborn," someone hissed. "She shouldn't even *exist*."

"Enough," the woman said, silencing them with a look. "She's not the enemy."

"She might not be," the younger man replied. "But *he* is."

Lyra's gaze snapped to him.

The man unrolled a faded parchment and tossed it onto the table.

Aris's face stared up at her.

Wanted.

Dead or alive.

Marked by the Order of the Silent as a traitor to the Fate Choir.

Lyra's breath hitched.

The woman watched her closely.

"You know him," she said softly.

Lyra didn't answer.

Couldn't.

"His name's Aris Caelen," the woman went on. "Former Threadblade. Once the Choir's favorite. Then their most dangerous failure."

Lyra stepped forward, drawn to the parchment. Her fingers hovered over his inked likeness.

Something deep inside her twisted.

The curve of his mouth. The scar beneath his left eye. She knew those things—not from recent memory, but from some deeper well of feeling.

"You remember," the woman said. Not unkindly.

Lyra looked up.

"He's the one who—" the man began.

"—cut the Anchor Thread," the woman finished. "Yes."

Gasps followed. Whispers.

"He severed the Loom," someone said. "Collapsed three timelines."

"Killed half the Weavers."

Lyra reeled.

The words crashed into her like waves against unsteady rock. They meant nothing. They meant *everything*.

She remembered his hands. The way they trembled when he touched her. The look in his eyes when he whispered her name.

Was that guilt?

She turned back to the woman.

The woman stepped closer.

"He was one of us once. Helped forge this rebellion. Gave us strategy, maps, names. Helped us survive the first wave of purges."

Lyra's head tilted.

"Then he vanished," she continued. "Right after silencing the girl who nearly ended the world."

Lyra's heart stopped.

She touched her own throat.

Realization sank in like a blade: *That girl was me.*

The room fell silent again.

The woman exhaled.

"My name is Lirael. I lead the Emberfold Rebellion. If you are who I think you are, you sang before the Silence fell. You were the final note before the collapse."

Lyra's hands shook.

Lirael caught her gently. "You don't have to remember everything. But if you remember *him*—you need to know what he chose."

The words pierced her.

Aris had saved her.

Aris had *betrayed* her.

Both things could be true.

And still—

Still, she felt the pull.

Not just of the thread that hummed beneath her skin.

But of *him*.

Somewhere beyond these caverns, Aris still walked the wilds with her name stitched into his pulse.

And something deep in the weave wanted them to meet again.

No—*needed* them to.

Lirael stepped back. "We'll give you time. But we'll also need to move. The Choir's hounds will come soon."

She turned and addressed the room.

"Prepare the spires. Ward the paths. She's under our protection now."

They moved quickly, vanishing into corridors and tunnels.

Lyra stood alone at the map table.

She touched Aris's face once more.

The pull inside her thrummed like a plucked string.

Memory.

Emotion.

Betrayal.

A future that hadn't happened yet, already unraveling.

And from the deepest part of the cave, the Looms began to *whisper*. Threads unseen but not silent. Her name echoed in their song.

And in the center of it all—beneath the layers of memory and lie—

Was his.

Aris.

The room felt smaller now, as though the walls themselves had drawn in to watch her, to wait. Lyra's fingers hovered above the parchment, tracing the edges of Aris's face in silence, the inked image almost a ghost beneath her touch. She could feel his presence in the trembling of her fingertips—familiar, yet foreign, like a dream that slips through your mind just as you wake.

Her heart beat erratically, a rhythm she couldn't quite place, but that she knew she had once felt before. She pulled her hand back, the coldness of the air stinging her skin, but it didn't numb the ache inside her chest.

"You've been with him," Lirael's voice interrupted her thoughts, quiet and firm. "You shared the same thread."

Lyra lifted her gaze to meet the woman's eyes, now more sympathetic than accusing. Lirael's dark eyes were calm, tempered with a lifetime of struggle and loss, but they held something else too—an understanding that made Lyra feel exposed.

"I… I don't remember," Lyra said, her voice barely above a whisper. She glanced at the map scattered with routes and lines, a tangled web of locations marked by faded symbols. It seemed wrong, to speak in that voice again—wrong to use her *real* voice after so long in silence. The words felt too heavy, as if the weight of them might crush her.

"You don't have to," Lirael said, coming to stand beside her. She reached out, placing a hand on Lyra's shoulder, grounding her. "But when the time comes, when you remember him, you need to choose. Because there will be no more running."

Lyra turned her head slowly, meeting Lirael's gaze. She could see the determination there, the force of someone who had long ago accepted the cost of rebellion, of war. Her words rang with the bitter truth of loss, of sacrifice. And somewhere beneath that bitterness—something darker—there was understanding. Lirael knew the truth of Aris's betrayal. She knew what it had cost.

"You already know what he did," Lirael continued, her voice low. "He *sacrificed* you. To stop the unraveling. To stop the destruction. But it wasn't just you, Lyra. He took that choice from you, and when he did, he shattered everything."

Lyra closed her eyes, breathing deeply. The weight of those words settled over her like a storm cloud. Her chest tightened. She didn't know if she could carry that knowledge, but it was true, wasn't it? She had been silenced for *their* safety, for the safety of the world, but at what cost? What had she lost?

And what had Aris lost in his choice?

The thread beneath her wrist pulsed again, an insistent beat, reminding her that no matter how much she wished it would go away, her connection to him was still alive, still woven into the very fabric of her existence.

Aris.

She breathed his name silently, feeling the weight of it draw the world closer to her.

"Do you remember the first time you saw him?" Lirael asked, her voice softer now, coaxing. "The first time he stood before you, when you had no idea what he would become?"

Lyra's mind went still.

The first time?

She thought—*felt*—the memory flicker. A blur. A memory behind a fog. She saw a young man, dressed in dark leathers, his eyes cold, distant. She saw a smile that hadn't reached his eyes, a sharp, secretive look that made her uneasy. And yet, somehow… she had trusted him. She had stood beside him, believing in him.

The memory vanished, too quickly, slipping from her fingers like water.

"I can't," Lyra whispered, blinking back tears that burned the edges of her vision. "I can't remember."

Lirael nodded, as if she'd expected the response, her hand still on Lyra's shoulder. "It will come back. The song will find its way to you again. But first, you must understand: you are not the only one who was changed that day. Aris *chose* the world, Lyra. But he also chose to bury you in silence."

"I know," Lyra murmured, closing her eyes tightly against the flood of grief that rose in her chest. "But he didn't want me to be forgotten."

Lirael's fingers tightened on her shoulder, a small gesture of solidarity. "No, he didn't. But his choices were made in haste.

He didn't think about what would happen to you after."

The door to the chamber creaked open then, interrupting their conversation. A man—one of the rebels, tall and wiry—stepped inside. His eyes were cautious, his steps silent, but Lyra could feel the shift in the air. The sense of unease in the room grew thicker, the shadows at the edge of her vision darkening.

"The Choir's scouts are getting closer," the man said, his voice tight. "They've spread through the eastern pass. We don't have much time."

Lirael turned sharply, her expression hardening. "We'll move tonight."

The man nodded, but his eyes flicked to Lyra, a silent acknowledgment of her presence. He didn't know her, not really. But they all knew the name she carried.

Lyra felt the weight of it—the name that had been stolen from her.

Her voice had been stolen.

Her choice had been taken.

And yet—

She was here.

She was *alive.*

The melody beneath her skin rose again, faint but clear.

Her song. Her voice.

Lyra inhaled sharply.

Lirael was speaking, but Lyra wasn't listening. Not really. Her attention had snapped to the door, to the shadow at the farthest corner of the room, where movement stirred.

She could hear it.

The faintest note—a whisper against the pull of the wind.

Aris.

She stood abruptly, the movement so sudden it startled the room.

"I have to go," Lyra said, her voice raw. "I need to find him."

Lirael's eyes softened, understanding flashing across her features, but her stance remained firm.

"No," she said, stepping forward. "We're moving tonight. You'll be safer with us. We need you."

Lyra shook her head, her heart pounding. "You don't understand. He's out there—somewhere. I can feel him. I need to see him. I need to know…"

The words stuck in her throat.

I need to know if he still remembers me.

Lirael studied her for a moment, then sighed. "Then let's go. But you'll have to move quickly."

Lyra nodded, the urgency pressing on her chest like a heavy stone. There was no more time. There was no more silence.

It was all unraveling.

As the rebels began to gather their things, moving swiftly but cautiously, Lyra stepped toward the doorway. Her hands shook at her sides, her pulse quickening.

But as she crossed the threshold, she felt it again.

The thread, pulling her forward.

Not just to him.

But toward something bigger.

Something older.

And more dangerous.

Lyra turned her head, scanning the distance.

Aris might not remember her.

But she would remember him.

And, this time, no one would steal her song.

The rebels scattered into the night, shadows blending into

the cold air. But Lyra stood at the edge, watching the horizon, waiting for the song to lead her back to him.

Five

A Name Forgotten, a Touch Remembered

The sky burned.

Not with fire, but with a deep crimson glow, as if the very heavens had been torn open, the bleeding wound exposed for the world to see. Aris stood at the edge of the plateau, watching the blood eclipse slowly swallow the moon. The air was thick, heavy with magic and the sharp tang of anticipation. A chill ran through him, not from the wind, but from the stirrings of something ancient, something *familiar*, shifting beneath his skin.

Tonight, the stars wouldn't guide them.

The sky, once a map for the Weavers, was darkened by the omen. The eclipse was not just a sign—it was a fracture. A sign that fate had been rewritten, twisted into something it was never meant to become.

He clenched his fists at his sides, resisting the compulsion to turn, to look behind him.

She was close now.

Lyra.

The name clung to him like a ghost.

He had felt her presence before he saw her—a pull in his chest, an ache deep within that had never truly gone away. His fingers twitched, a silent plea to reach for something long lost. He'd betrayed her. He had severed their bond, silenced her voice, buried the memory of who she was and what she had meant to him.

And yet…

And yet, she was here.

In the darkness. In the *silence*.

Aris could feel the weight of her gaze before she stepped into the clearing. Her silhouette emerged from the shadows, the faint glow of the eclipse casting her in a soft, unnatural light. She was *changed*, but then again, so was he. Time had aged them both—grief had worn their bodies, but it was the soul that bore the heaviest scars.

Her eyes locked with his. Dark, stormy. Her hair shimmered like silver thread woven into night.

He took a slow step forward.

But no words came.

No *memory*—not one that could be trusted.

She was silent too, her lips parted as if ready to speak, but her voice, *her voice*, was nowhere to be found. Just the faintest breath between them. A void that stretched farther than the distance between them.

The eclipse deepened. The wind began to stir, a soft rustling sound that filled the silence between them, making the air feel thick and alive.

Lyra's gaze flickered to his hand. She took a hesitant step toward him, drawn to the thread of fate pulsing faintly beneath his skin. He could feel it—the magnetic pull of her presence, the fragile, shimmering thread that connected them even now. As she neared, his heart seemed to beat faster, as if his blood was waking from a long slumber. Her steps faltered when she reached him, her fingers hovering just inches from his own.

He swallowed, forcing the words that had long been buried to surface. "Lyra…" His voice cracked.

Her breath hitched, a flicker of recognition passing over her features—faint, fleeting—but enough to tear at his chest. He reached out without thinking, his hand catching hers.

The moment their skin made contact, the world around them seemed to tremble. The eclipse reached its zenith, and the ground beneath their feet vibrated with an energy neither of them could explain.

For a moment, neither of them spoke. Neither of them moved.

The silence shattered between them like glass.

A flood of sensation crashed through them, a tidal wave of memory, emotion, and *touch*. It was as if the air itself had turned to song, and beneath the weight of it, the fractured pieces of their shared past snapped back into place.

The first kiss.

The first war.

The last moment they had shared, before it all fell apart.

Lyra's chest tightened, her breath shallow as the memories overwhelmed her. Aris staggered back, his heart pounding in his ears. He closed his eyes, his fingers tightening around hers.

And then—the kiss.

It was not just a memory.

It was *their* kiss.

Her lips against his. Their hearts beating together in rhythm. The world falling away, leaving only the pull of fate, of song. Her hands on his shoulders, his arms around her waist, drawing her closer, as if no force could tear them apart.

But something *did*. Something broke them. Something that neither could prevent.

A cry.

A scream.

A rift.

The light of the eclipse flared around them, blinding, and in the brief flash of brilliance, everything went dark again.

Lyra stumbled, her chest rising and falling with the remnants of the vision. The memory had nearly consumed them both. She pulled her hand away, her gaze wild as she tried to make sense of what she had just experienced. Her fingers trembled.

"What was that?" she whispered, her voice cracking with the weight of the question.

Aris stared at her, chest rising and falling, his mind still reeling from the rush of memories. "It's… it's us," he said hoarsely. "It's the *song*."

She shook her head, trying to clear the fog. "I don't… I don't remember you. Not like that."

His heart clenched. "I know. I know you don't."

There was a deep ache in his voice, a rawness that came from years of regret, years of forcing the truth down into a place where it couldn't be touched.

She stepped back, her eyes wide, searching his face. "Why… Why didn't you tell me? Why did you silence me?"

The question tore through him like a blade. He reached for her, but the distance between them felt like a chasm that stretched far beyond the physical. She was right. She *deserved* the truth. But he had buried it so deeply, even from himself, that he hadn't known how to begin to unravel it.

"Because I thought… I thought it would be better for you," he said, his voice low and unsteady. "Because the threads were breaking, and your voice… your power… it was too much. It was too dangerous, Lyra. I—I thought I was saving you from it." His voice broke on the last words, the truth of it all crashing over him like a wave.

She stood there, silent, her chest rising and falling in slow, measured breaths. Her gaze never left his.

"I never asked you to save me," she whispered. "I never asked you to *take* my voice. My memories."

The words hung between them, and for the first time in years, Aris felt the weight of his betrayal in full force. Not just for what he had done to her, but for what it had done to *him*. To them.

He took a step toward her, his hand reaching for hers, but the thread that had once bound them was no longer the same. The silence, though broken, still lingered between them. A fragile, uncertain thing.

"I'm sorry," he said, the words so simple, so inadequate.

She looked at him for a long moment, her lips parted as if to say something more, but she stopped. She lowered her gaze, turning away as the eclipse waned, the blood-red moon beginning to fade.

"I don't know if I can forgive you," she said quietly, her voice breaking with emotion. "But I know we need each other now. I know there's no running from this."

Aris swallowed hard. His heart was heavy, but in that moment, something new began to take root—something small, fragile, but undeniable.

She didn't trust him yet.

But *she was still here.*

And for the first time in years, he allowed himself to believe in the possibility of redemption, of a future.

The silence had broken. But not entirely.

And there were still threads of fate to weave.

The last of the eclipse faded into the night sky, leaving behind a darkened world where both memory and fate hung in the balance.

The silence between them stretched on, thick and heavy, as if the world itself was waiting for them to speak. The last of the eclipse vanished, its blood-red glow retreating into the black sky, leaving only the pale light of the stars. The air, once crackling with energy, now seemed muted, as if the very night had drawn a breath and held it, uncertain of what came next.

Lyra stood at the edge of the clearing, her back to him, shoulders tense as though she was holding herself together by sheer force of will. Aris watched her, his heart in his throat, unable to move. The weight of her words—her pain—hung like a shackle around him. He wanted to reach for her, to make her understand, to undo the damage he had done.

But every time he took a step forward, the distance between them felt impossible to cross.

"I never wanted to silence you," he said at last, his voice hoarse. "I thought I was saving you from something far worse. I thought—" His words faltered. He took a breath, trying to steady himself. "I thought if I kept you away from the Weave, from the power you held, you'd be safe. That it would protect you."

Lyra turned then, her eyes dark, searching his face for the truth she had long since buried beneath layers of distrust and pain. "Safe?" Her voice was quiet, but there was a sharp edge to it, like the sting of an old wound reopening. "I was never safe, Aris. Not from the beginning. And now... now I don't know who I am anymore."

The weight of her gaze hit him like a physical blow. He closed his eyes for a moment, the realization of everything he had taken from her—her memories, her voice, her autonomy— settling in like a crushing weight.

"I thought... I thought you would forgive me," he murmured, stepping closer. "That you would understand why I did it."

Lyra's eyes flicked to his hand, the one still outstretched toward her. For a long, agonizing moment, she said nothing. She didn't pull away, but she didn't move toward him either. She stood frozen, caught between what she remembered and what she was too afraid to face.

"I don't even know what *this* is anymore," she said softly. "The song we shared, the bond between us... it's broken. I don't know if I can ever go back to what we were."

The words sliced through him like a dagger, and for a moment, he thought he might collapse under the weight of it. What *were* they now? What *had* they been, if not a web of lies, manipulation, and silence?

He swallowed the bitter taste in his mouth and took a step closer, his eyes never leaving hers. "Lyra, I've never stopped loving you. Even when I thought I was saving you, I was wrong. I *knew* I was wrong, but I couldn't stop it. Not when I saw the way the world was falling apart. Not when I saw what your power could do."

She flinched at the words, her eyes flicking to the ground,

her fingers curling into fists at her sides. "My power? My power almost *destroyed* everything, Aris. You didn't stop me. You *took* it from me. You took *me* from myself."

The words burned, each syllable an ember that left a scar. Aris's throat tightened. "I never meant to take you from you," he said, his voice trembling. "I only wanted to protect you. But I see now… I see what I've done."

She lifted her gaze to him, her eyes raw with hurt and confusion. "Then why didn't you trust me?"

He hesitated.

"I was *afraid*," he admitted, his voice barely above a whisper. "I was afraid of losing you, of losing everything. I saw the way the threads unraveled around us, and I couldn't bear the thought of you being swallowed by it."

Lyra's eyes softened, just for a moment. A flicker of the girl he once knew—so full of fire, of light—shone through the shadow. But it was fleeting. Like everything between them now, fragile and slipping through their fingers.

"I wanted to *save* you," he said again, almost pleading, as if his heart could convince her in ways his words never could. "I didn't want to see you lost in the Weave, like everyone else."

"You should have let me choose," Lyra replied, her voice steady but full of pain. "I would have chosen differently."

The silence that followed was suffocating.

And then—

The ground trembled beneath their feet.

Lyra gasped, her hand instinctively reaching for Aris as the earth shook again, stronger this time. The trees above them groaned as if the very world was waking from a long slumber. The thread on his wrist pulsed violently, as though it, too, sensed the disturbance. Aris's heart skipped a beat as he looked toward the horizon.

A figure emerged from the trees.

Tall, cloaked in shadows, with eyes that burned through the dark like the heat of a thousand suns.

The Voidborn.

A single, dark shape, standing at the edge of the clearing, its body made of shifting shadows. It was the same creature from the forest—its form incomplete, flickering like a flame about to be snuffed out. And in its hollow, featureless face, Lyra saw something she hadn't noticed before—an echo of *her* song.

The creature spoke then, its voice an eerie echo that slid through the air like silk and glass.

"You can't escape what you are," it said, its voice low and resonant, vibrating through their bones. "Not from *her.*"

Aris moved instinctively, pulling Lyra behind him, his hand going for the dagger at his side. But the creature didn't attack. Instead, it spoke again, this time in a voice that mimicked Lyra's own.

"*You will sing him into ash,*" it whispered, the words twisting through the air like a snake. "*As you did once before.*"

Lyra's breath caught in her throat.

She stepped forward, her hands shaking, but not from fear. It was something else—something deeper, darker, like the call of a song buried too long. She took a step closer to the creature.

"No," she said, her voice stronger now, her own. "I am not the same."

The creature tilted its head, its empty eyes fixating on her. "You can't run from the melody," it murmured. "It will consume you, just as it consumes everything else."

Lyra stood tall, her chest rising with every breath. The silence, once a prison, was no longer as terrifying. She had felt it, that touch—the remnants of their bond. It was still there, flickering, waiting. It wasn't gone. Not yet.

She reached for the air, the thread beneath her skin singing faintly, drawing a line from her to Aris. A thread that should never have been severed.

And as her fingers closed around the space between them, she felt it again.

The pull. The bond. The *song.*

Her eyes met Aris's. And for a brief, fleeting moment, the world shifted—time rewound, and the memory of their first kiss came crashing back.

Not as a dream.

But as a reality, one they could still reach for.

"I won't let you silence me," she said, her voice rising, louder now.

The ground rumbled again, and the creature screamed. The sound split the air—sharp, discordant.

But Lyra's song rose louder.

And for the first time in years, she felt the threads of fate weave around her—not as chains, but as something *alive.*

And in the midst of it, she reached for Aris.

Their fingers touched.

The silence broke.

Six

Threads That Bleed

The moon hung low over the valley, casting a silvered sheen over the landscape, its light both eerie and ethereal. The wind had stilled, leaving the air thick and heavy with anticipation. Aris stood at the edge of the clearing, watching Lyra as she paced quietly, her face tense, her hands clasped tightly in front of her. Her eyes never left the horizon, as if she could feel it coming—just as he could.

There was no time left.

They had been running for days now, moving swiftly through the abandoned paths, avoiding the Order of the Silent, staying hidden. But Aris could feel the pressure building, the weight of something greater pressing down on them, something older and darker than even the Order.

He turned his head slightly, his eyes narrowing as the wind picked up once more, this time carrying something with it. A smell. Not of earth or leaves, but of something darker, colder.

The scent of death.

A shadow moved at the edge of the clearing.

Aris's heart stopped.

The wind shifted, and the faintest whisper of a voice reached his ears. It was low, cold, and unmistakably familiar.

"Lyra Elowen…"

The voice was like steel scraping against stone. It cut through the silence of the night with a finality that left no room for escape.

Aris's hand flew to the hilt of his dagger, the blade still fresh from their previous skirmish. But this time, there would be no dodging fate. The creature that stepped from the darkness wasn't just a mere assassin. It was a Fate-Reaper. And it had come for *her*.

Lyra froze, her eyes widening. Aris saw the flash of fear cross her face, but it was quickly replaced by a fierce resolve. She had changed since the first time they met—the quiet, vulnerable girl from the glade was now a woman of strength, of *power*. Still, the weight of what stood before them made the ground beneath him feel unstable.

The Fate-Reaper stepped into the clearing, its long cloak billowing around it, its face hidden beneath a dark mask. Its presence felt like the last moment before a storm, an inevitability that was both terrifying and magnetic.

"You are the last Threadborn," the Reaper intoned, its voice a deep, guttural echo. "You should never have survived. You should never have been allowed to return."

Lyra's gaze flicked to Aris, her eyes pleading silently with him. She didn't need to ask. He could already see the storm gathering in her eyes. She knew what was at stake.

Aris took a slow, measured breath, his hand tightening

around the dagger. His heart pounded, not from fear, but from something more primal. Something older.

"I won't let you take her," he growled, his voice low, a warning in itself.

The Fate-Reaper tilted its head, and for a brief moment, Aris thought it might be considering him—*calculating*. Its gaze seemed to pierce right through him, as if it could see every fault, every regret that lingered in his soul.

"You *cannot* protect her," the Reaper said, its voice filled with an unearthly calm. "The threads have already begun to unravel, and she is the final knot. She will be erased from this world, and fate will correct itself."

Lyra took a step forward, her fists clenched. "I am not some *knot* to be erased."

The Reaper's hand shot out with unnatural speed, grabbing her by the wrist. Aris moved, but it was too fast. The creature's strength was like iron, cold and unyielding, and Lyra winced as the grip tightened.

"She is not to be saved," the Reaper whispered, its cold breath like ice on her skin. "She is a mistake, a fissure in the fabric of fate. And you—" It turned its empty, black gaze on Aris, the chill of it almost freezing him in place. "You have been the fool to try and protect it."

Aris felt a surge of rage, a heat that rose from his chest, but it was no use. The creature was too strong, too ancient. His thread—whatever remained of it—was no match for the Reaper's power.

But then—

The thread beneath his wrist pulsed.

A sudden, fierce pull, so strong it made him stumble. His chest constricted, and in that moment, he realized something—

something horrifying.

He could feel it.

The last of his remaining thread—the one that had bound him to Lyra—was calling him.

It was not just a connection between them. It was a *bond*.

A bond that, in this moment, could be the only weapon he had.

Aris drew in a sharp breath. He didn't think. Didn't hesitate.

He tore the thread from his wrist.

The pain was blinding.

His entire body shuddered as if every nerve was being ripped apart at once. His vision blurred. His chest burned with the effort of it. But the moment the last of the thread left his body, the world around him snapped into focus.

Lyra's scream filled his ears, sharp and high-pitched, but it was distant, as if coming from underwater. The Fate-Reaper had loosened its grip on her, but only just enough to allow Aris to close the distance.

With a single motion, Aris thrust his hands into the air, forcing the energy that remained of his thread into the space between them. His vision blurred again, but this time with purpose, as his power—the final fragments of his bond with Lyra—unraveled. The thread became something else. Something darker.

The thread burned.

It lashed out like a living thing, wrapping around the Fate-Reaper's limbs, tangling it in a web of raw energy. The Reaper howled in pain, its mask cracking under the pressure. Its form shimmered, flickering, as though it could not exist in the space between the worlds where Aris was pulling it.

"You *will* not take her," Aris gritted out, his voice strained as the pain in his chest grew unbearable.

The creature struggled, thrashing against the power of the thread, but it was too late. The last of Aris's bond snapped into place, binding them both—him and the Reaper. The thread became a chain, locking them together.

The Fate-Reaper's form crumbled, its edges blurring as if time itself was unraveling around it. It screamed again, this time in a language no mortal should ever hear, before its body collapsed into the ground, turning to dust before Aris's very eyes.

Silence fell.

For a moment, neither Aris nor Lyra moved. Aris's chest heaved, every muscle in his body screaming in pain. The thread had been his last anchor to reality, and now, it was gone. Nothing remained.

He turned to Lyra, his vision swimming, his breath ragged. He had given everything. He had sacrificed the last piece of himself to save her.

But the silence between them was still there.

And it *hurt*.

Lyra's face was pale, her eyes wide with disbelief as she stared at the ashes where the Fate-Reaper had once stood.

She opened her mouth to speak, but nothing came out.

The thread. The bond. The magic—they were gone. And now, they were just two souls, standing in a world that had once been theirs.

Aris took a step toward her, his hand shaking as he reached for her, but Lyra stepped back.

"I... I can't..." she whispered, shaking her head. "What have you done?"

Her words were like daggers, each one twisting deeper into

his chest.

He had given up the last of his thread, the last of his magic, to protect her.

But it wasn't enough.

He wasn't enough.

Her eyes glistened with tears, but she didn't move toward him. She didn't reach for him. She stood frozen, her hands trembling at her sides.

Aris took another step forward, his voice broken. "Lyra… please…"

But she couldn't hear him. Not anymore.

The last thread of their bond had *bled*.

And now, the world was silent.

And the darkness was closing in.

The wind howled across the desolate valley, a constant scream that tore at the earth. Lyra shivered, wrapping her cloak tighter around her shoulders, though the cold wasn't from the wind. No, it was the heavy, unnatural silence that hung over them. The world felt wrong, a jagged edge of tension cutting through the air, as if the very fabric of reality had started to fray.

They had stopped to rest in the remnants of a crumbled tower, its stones long weathered and crumbling from years of neglect. A distant fire flickered in the distance, the embers faint in the dying light. Aris had built it carefully, just enough to warm the night, just enough to mask their presence in the cold shadows. It was, he hoped, far enough from the Order, far enough from the creatures that hunted them.

But the weight of the stillness grew heavier with every passing moment.

Lyra stood by the edge of the ruin, her hands still trembling, her breath shallow. The thread on her wrist pulsed with every breath, a reminder of the power she had no control over, a reminder of the weight of their shared fate. She could feel it—the constant hum that ran through her, vibrating in the air. The threads of time, the very essence of fate itself, weaving together to create something larger than them both.

Behind her, Aris was silent, but she could feel him too—just as she felt the pull of the thread. He was standing by the fire, his back turned, hands folded across his chest. She could feel the quiet sorrow in him, a resignation that hadn't been there before.

The world felt like it was holding its breath.

Then, the earth moved.

The first tremor was small—a slight shudder that sent a ripple through the stone beneath her feet. Lyra glanced over her shoulder, her heart picking up speed. Aris tensed, his hands balling into fists. He knew it too.

"Get down," he ordered sharply, his voice low.

Before she could respond, a shadow fell over them. It was like the sun had suddenly dipped below the horizon, leaving only the crushing weight of the darkness behind.

And then she saw it.

A figure emerged from the shadows, impossibly tall, draped in dark, flowing robes that shimmered like liquid night. A Fate-Reaper. Its face was obscured by a mask—a gleaming, reflective surface that showed nothing but the emptiness of the world. No eyes. No features. Just the mask, staring straight through her. The figure moved with an unnerving silence, its presence pressing down on her chest, suffocating her.

Aris's hand shot out, grabbing her wrist and pulling her back into the shadows of the ruins. "Don't move," he hissed.

But Lyra couldn't look away. The Fate-Reaper's presence was too overwhelming, too vast, too deep. She could feel the weight of its gaze, even without eyes to see her. It was a thing of death, of endings, of *destinies severed.*

And it had come for her.

"Lyra Elowen," the voice spoke, not loud but still so full of authority, so full of power, that it rang in her ears. *"The last Threadborn."*

Her heart stopped.

The last? The *last?*

The Reaper stepped forward, its robes sweeping across the ground in ripples. "You are an anomaly," it continued, its voice cold as ice. "A break in the Weave. A mistake that must be corrected. Your power was never meant to exist. Your fate was sealed long ago."

Aris stepped in front of Lyra, his body tensed, his face pale. "You're not taking her."

The Fate-Reaper's head tilted ever so slightly, and the sound that followed was like the shifting of an ancient, cursed stone. It did not speak again for a long moment.

"You cannot stop what is already written, *Aris Caelen,*" it said, its voice ringing with finality. "You have broken the threads, but there is one thread left. And it is *hers.*"

Aris's hand twitched, as if he were reaching for something. Lyra's eyes flickered to him, but she couldn't read his expression. She couldn't read anything in the darkening space between them.

And then, the Fate-Reaper moved.

It extended one long, unnaturally thin hand, and the space around them seemed to warp, the very air bending under the pressure. Lyra gasped, her feet slipping as the earth trembled again. The air thickened with the scent of decay, of death and time unraveling.

"No!" Aris shouted, stepping forward and pulling Lyra back into the stone shadows. But it was too late.

The Reaper's hand shot forward, a silver thread extending from its palm, glowing faintly in the dim light. It was a thread of death, a thread that could sever the soul itself. Aris's breath caught in his throat, his eyes wide with understanding. He had no time to draw his blade, no time to protect her.

Lyra screamed—but no sound came. The thread snapped toward her.

In that instant, something broke inside her.

Something *awoke*.

Her heart pounded in her chest, her fingers clutching the thread on her wrist. Her magic—her power—surged, not as a whisper, but as a roar. Light exploded from her chest, brilliant and blinding. She could feel the song, the Weave, the *thread of her being* vibrating through her, pulsing with energy, with fate.

The silver thread that the Fate-Reaper had cast shattered. The light, her light, sliced through the air, cutting through the Reaper's thread as if it were paper.

But as the light reached its peak, it faltered. The energy dissipated, the thread around her wrist snapping like a taut string. Her legs gave out beneath her, and she collapsed to the ground, gasping for air.

Aris was at her side in an instant, his hands reaching for her, his voice frantic. "Lyra! Lyra, stay with me!"

She could barely hear him. The edges of her vision were clouding, her breath coming in shallow gasps. The world tilted. She reached for him instinctively, her hand trembling, and for the briefest moment, her fingers brushed his.

The thread on her wrist flickered once, then again. Her power hummed faintly, alive again, but weakened, strained.

The Fate-Reaper turned, its head tilting again as if contemplating their feeble attempt to fight back. The figure stepped closer, its mask reflecting the night, gleaming with a malevolent light.

"I warned you," it said softly, as though it had no emotion, no intention to kill—only to erase. "The Threadborn cannot live. The threads *must* be severed."

Lyra's body was frozen, every muscle screaming as the world around her started to blur, but then—

Aris was standing in front of her. His back to her, his body trembling with unspoken resolve.

"No," he said, voice thick with desperation. "Not like this. You won't take her."

The Reaper regarded him for a long moment, its hand rising again, the thread already forming in the air.

But Aris's eyes—dark, wide with fear and resolve—flashed toward her.

"I won't let them take you," he muttered, his voice rough with pain. "I won't let you be erased."

Before Lyra could stop him, before the world could close in around them, he reached down to his own wrist.

The thread that had once been his—the one that bound him to everything he had ever fought for, everything he had loved— glowed faintly in the dim light. He ripped it free with a brutal motion, and the fabric of his fate unraveled in front of them.

Lyra gasped.

"Aris, no!" she whispered, her voice coming back in a choking sob.

But it was too late.

The thread snapped in two.

The moment it did, the air shifted, the ground beneath them trembled violently, and the world seemed to stop breathing. The Reaper's mask flickered, the seams of its existence starting to unravel as the bond between Aris and Lyra was reforged. Their fates entwined.

The light from Lyra's wrist flared brightly, consuming the space between them, igniting the darkness.

In the Reaper's last moments, its mask shattered with a hiss, the threads of fate it had been drawing unraveling completely as the force of Aris's sacrifice collided with the weight of the world.

Lyra's breath caught in her throat.

She reached for him—fingers outstretched—but the threads between them were still not yet strong enough to hold. They were still bleeding, unraveling.

And the Void, once silent, began to stir.

The air hung thick with the echoes of Aris's sacrifice. The world around them was frozen in a moment of tension so tight it felt like the fabric of reality itself might snap. The land trembled beneath their feet, the earth groaning as if in response to the force of Aris's final act. The light from Lyra's wrist, the energy she had once feared, now surged with a life of its own.

But it wasn't enough.

Not yet.

Lyra's breath came in shallow gasps as she reached for Aris, her fingers trembling in the dim light. She couldn't feel his thread anymore. The bond they had once shared, the last thread that had bound them together, was gone. She didn't know what was left of him—what was left of *her*—but she had to try. She couldn't let him slip away.

Her fingers brushed his arm, the contact jolting through her like a bolt of lightning.

"Aris," she whispered, her voice strained, desperate. "Please… please don't leave me."

The faintest breath of wind stirred, lifting the edges of her cloak, but Aris didn't stir. His body was limp, his eyes closed. His pulse—barely there—throbbed weakly beneath his skin, like the last remnants of a fading star.

Lyra's chest tightened, her heart aching with something far more painful than grief. There was nothing left. No more magic. No more bond. Only the hollow emptiness where their fates had once been woven together.

And then—just as the weight of the Void pressed down on her, threatening to swallow them both—

Aris's hand twitched.

Lyra's breath caught.

Her hands shot to his, pressing against his cold skin. She held him tighter, willing him to wake, to come back, to *feel her* again. She could still feel the warmth of the thread that had bound them—deep inside her, in places she hadn't known were still alive. It was *there*, faint, but not gone entirely. It flickered weakly, like a dying flame, but it was something—something she could hold onto.

A low rumble vibrated through the air, a dark, ominous sound that came not from the ground, but from the very *void* itself. The sky above them darkened, the blood-red moon now shrouded by a creeping cloud of blackness. It was as if the world had exhaled its final breath.

Then, the shadows moved.

Not as one, but in *unison*—as if something ancient, something *alive*, was stirring beneath the surface of the land.

Aris stirred again.

Lyra's heart leaped into her throat, her hands shaking. He was breathing more steadily now, though his breaths were shallow and weak. She could feel him beginning to return—*to her*. But something was wrong. She could sense it. The very threads of the world were unraveling, spiraling out of control, and the Void was only moments away from consuming them all.

"Aris," she breathed, her voice barely a whisper, "you have to wake up. Please, I need you."

The wind howled once more, and with it, the unmistakable presence of the Void moved closer. The earth beneath her trembled with an unnatural pulse—a deep, resonating vibration that rippled through her very soul. She could hear the faintest echo of a song. Not a song of light, not a song of life, but of *destruction*.

The Void was coming.

And it was not just a force of nature—it was a force *determined* to consume what remained of the Weave, of fate itself.

With a final, desperate effort, Lyra pressed her forehead to Aris's, her breath mingling with his as she willed the last of her power to return. She reached for the threads that remained, the faint, fraying strands of their connection that had once bound their fates together. She closed her eyes, willing everything she had left to surge through her, to reconnect what had been severed.

But it wasn't enough.

A voice, deep and ancient, echoed through her mind.

"You have only delayed the inevitable, Threadborn."

It was the voice of the Void. Not a whisper, but a presence—

suffocating, all-encompassing. It swept through her, blocking out her thoughts, drowning out her will. It reached for her, wrapping its unseen fingers around her heart.

She gritted her teeth, feeling the pressure build, the force of the Void pulling at her very essence, threatening to tear her apart.

And yet, in the darkness, she felt it.

A pulse.

A thread, *barely alive*, but *alive nonetheless*.

Aris's hand, still limp in hers, twitched again. This time, more strongly.

The Void recoiled.

A surge of power rippled through the air, making the trees around them tremble, their leaves rustling in unnatural whispers. The air grew colder, and the pressure lifted just enough for Lyra to take a breath.

"Aris," she whispered, her voice breaking. She pressed her hands to his chest, feeling the faint, fragile thrum of life beneath her palms. "I need you… I need you now."

In that moment, she felt it—a flicker of their bond, a surge of shared memory that came not from the thread, but from something deeper. Something older. The song they had once sung together, the bond they had once shared, was still within them. It was *in them*, not as a thread, but as a living, breathing force that could not die—not completely.

And then, with a burst of energy, Aris's eyes snapped open.

The world seemed to stop.

For a moment, neither of them moved. Lyra stared at him, her heart racing, her hands still pressed against his chest. His eyes were wide, filled with confusion, pain, and—something else.

Recognition.

He blinked, as if trying to make sense of the world around him.

"Lyra," he rasped, his voice rough with strain. "I… I can't—"

"You're here," she said, her voice breaking as tears filled her eyes. "You're *here*. Please, please stay with me."

But even as she spoke, the pressure in the air began to return.

The Void was not gone.

The dark shape that had emerged from the shadows was now looming above them, its presence pressing down like a weight on their chests.

"I told you," the Void said, its voice a low, mocking whisper. "You cannot escape fate. You cannot stop what has been written."

Lyra's heart raced as she turned her gaze to the Voidborn, her breath shallow. Aris's grip on her hand tightened, his fingers cold but steady.

"Aris," she whispered, her voice urgent. "The thread… it's still there. I can feel it. *You* can still fight. You can still save us."

His eyes flickered with something—something she hadn't seen in him for so long. Something alive. Something *familiar*.

"We can't let it win," Aris said, his voice steadying, the strength returning to him. His hand reached for hers, his fingers wrapping around her wrist. The thread beneath their skin pulsed again, stronger this time, as if responding to the presence of the Void.

Lyra closed her eyes, letting the connection between them flood her senses once more. This was no longer a bond of magic, no longer just a thread. This was something *deeper*. Something *stronger*.

They had only moments.

But this time, they would not be broken.

Together, they stood.

And together, they would fight.

The Void had come for them both. But it would not take them without a fight. And this time, there would be no escape.

Only the storm.

And the silence that followed it.

Seven

The Songless Pact

The citadel was falling apart.

Aris could feel it, the weight of the world shifting beneath his feet. The very stones beneath him trembled as if the ancient walls were gasping for air, struggling to keep themselves intact. The screams of the dying citadel echoed through the halls, vibrating through the cracks in the stone. Dust hung thick in the air, swirling like fog, stinging his eyes, thickening with each passing second. The flames that had ravaged the outer walls now crept closer, licking the edges of the grand archways and towers.

It wouldn't be long.

Lyra was still beside him, her hand clutching his, her breath shaky but steady as they navigated through the crumbling corridors. The once-pristine tapestries that had adorned the walls were now nothing more than charred remnants, their threads dissolving into smoke. Her face was pale, eyes wide, reflecting the light of the fire outside, but there was something else behind them—a deep, flickering fire of resolve.

The song that had once thrummed in her soul, the one that could reshape the very fabric of fate, was no longer singing as it once had. That was the price they had paid. The bond they had forged had tied their fates together, but in doing so, it had silenced the echoes of her voice. The magic within her, the raw power that had once bent reality itself, was fading, slipping away with each passing breath. But she was still here.

Still with him.

And now, they had one chance left.

The citadel, once a symbol of power, was now a death trap. The last of the Weavers were dead, the Chorus scattered, and the remnants of the Order had long since abandoned their posts, leaving only the hushed whispers of their failures behind. But Aris had one card left to play. One last chance to keep them both alive. One last desperate gamble that would bind them, heart and soul, to escape the collapse.

Lyra stopped suddenly, her fingers tightening around his.

"Aris," she breathed, her voice quiet but urgent. "We don't have much time."

He turned to face her, his chest tightening at the sight of her. There was so much he wanted to say, so much he needed to explain, but the words caught in his throat. He could see it in her eyes—the same resolve that had driven her to fight for him, for their shared future, even when it seemed impossible. The same resolve that had shattered their past, leaving only the broken fragments of a world they no longer recognized.

The air around them was thick with the weight of their decisions, the sacrifices they had made to reach this point.

"I know," he whispered, squeezing her hand. "I know, Lyra.

But this is the only way."

She met his gaze, her eyes searching his, as if looking for the truth in the space between them. The space that had once been filled with their shared songs, their dreams, their bond. Now, it was only silence.

"You're asking me to give it all up," she said, her voice shaking with emotion. "My voice… my power. Everything that makes me—me."

"I'm asking you to save us," Aris said, his voice steady, though his heart was beating faster than he cared to admit. "If we don't do this, the citadel will collapse. The threads will unravel, and everything we've fought for will be lost. You're the last one who can stop it."

Her eyes softened for a moment, the battle within her plain to see. She had always been the one to fight, to push forward, no matter the cost. But this was different. This wasn't a battle with an enemy. This was a fight with herself. A fight to decide how much of herself she was willing to sacrifice to save them both.

"I can't—" Her voice cracked, the weight of her decision pressing down on her chest. "I can't lose it. I can't lose *everything*."

"I know," Aris whispered. "But you won't lose everything. You'll still have *me*."

The words were soft, almost lost in the chaos around them. But they were enough. Enough to steady her. Enough to give her the courage to do what needed to be done.

Lyra turned away, her fingers still gripping his tightly, her breath shaky as she looked at the crumbling walls, the flames licking at the edges of the sky.

The room around them felt smaller, tighter, like the walls

were closing in. The heat of the fire grew stronger, its crackling reaching into the corners of their minds. Aris knew there was no more time. The collapse of the citadel was inevitable. If they didn't act now, if they didn't bind their fates, they would be swallowed by the darkness that was already consuming everything.

"Lyra," Aris said softly, reaching for her again. She looked up at him, her eyes wide with the weight of the decision before her. "We can't stop it unless we do this. You have to give up your voice. Just for a moment. For us. For the future."

The silence between them deepened as she searched his face, her heart beating faster with each passing second. She wanted to say something, to argue, but the truth was clear. She had no choice. Not anymore. If she didn't sacrifice this part of herself, they would both be lost.

With a final, shuddering breath, she nodded.

"I'll do it."

Aris's heart twisted as he watched her. She had always been strong, but in this moment, she was more vulnerable than he had ever seen her. The magic that surged between them had been powerful, but it had also been dangerous. The threads that connected their fates had been weakened by the battles they had fought, the choices they had made. And now, they would be bound in a new way—a way that neither of them fully understood, but that they both had to trust.

Lyra closed her eyes, her hands trembling as she lifted them to her chest, where the thread once pulsed with the power of her song. The air around them seemed to tighten, like the very walls of the citadel were holding their breath.

"Aris," she whispered, her voice soft but filled with strength. "I trust you."

Without another word, she began to unravel the thread—the magic that had been growing in her since the moment she had touched Aris's hand. She knew what she had to do. She had to sever it, let it go. The song that had once filled her soul, the voice that had once been the key to everything, was now fading. She could feel it, like a weight pulling at her heart, but she had no choice. She had to give it up.

Her fingers traced the line of magic, the thread that had once been a part of her, until it broke free. The world around her trembled as the power surged through her, but she didn't resist. She let it go, watched as it unraveled before her.

The silence deepened.

The moment the thread was severed, the world seemed to pause.

Lyra gasped, feeling the weight of the silence pressing against her chest, suffocating her. She couldn't hear anything anymore. Not the crackling of the fire. Not the rush of wind outside. Only the thudding of her own heart in the emptiness.

And then, Aris was there. His hand found hers, his warmth flooding through her like a lifeline. His voice was soft, steady, but it filled the silence.

"We're still here," he said. "We're still together."

But Lyra didn't feel the connection. Not like she had before. The thread was gone. The song was gone. And yet, something in her shifted. Something deep, beneath the weight of the silence, stirred. She was still *her*, but the *us* she had known— the bond she had once held between them— was now only a faint memory.

The collapse of the citadel was still coming.

And they were still bound by fate.

But the song, the voice that had carried them through the

darkest moments, was now gone.

The silence was thick, suffocating.

And in the deepening dark, the world outside called to them—darkness, void, and the things that waited to consume the remnants of their broken fates.

But for now, there was only the silence.

And the pact they had made.

And the world that was slowly falling apart around them.

The silence stretched between them, thicker than the walls of the citadel, heavier than the crumbling stone beneath their feet. Lyra's breath felt ragged, as if every inhalation was forced, every exhale pushing against the stillness that had settled in the space around them. The world had shifted—the song, the magic that had once defined her, was gone. But the echo of it lingered, faint and distant, as though a part of her had been severed, and now only a hollow shell remained.

Aris's hand in hers was the only tether left, the only reminder that the world hadn't completely unraveled yet. His grip was tight, reassuring, but Lyra could feel the tremble in his fingers, the unspoken fear in the way he held her. He was holding on, too, but for reasons she couldn't quite grasp. He wasn't just holding on to her. He was holding on to something else— something fragile that was slipping through their fingers.

Aris had made the choice. He had forced the bond between them, a sacrifice of everything he had left to protect her. But in doing so, he had torn them apart, just as surely as the threads had been severed.

"I'm sorry," she whispered, her voice raspy, unfamiliar without the melody that once filled her soul. It felt like a stranger's voice now, harsh and foreign, nothing like the soft, lilting tones she had once used to weave the world into existence.

Aris turned toward her, his face shadowed in the dim light of the crumbling citadel, his eyes searching hers. He said nothing at first, but his gaze softened, and his hand moved to cup her cheek.

"You don't have to apologize," he said, his voice steady despite the weight of the situation. "You did what you had to. We did what we had to."

Lyra shook her head, her eyes stinging with the emotion that swelled inside her chest. "But I… I lost it, Aris. Everything I've been fighting for. Everything I've been trying to protect. It's gone now."

"Not everything," he replied, his thumb brushing lightly against her skin, as if trying to erase the distance between them. "You're still here. We're still here. And we still have time."

Her breath caught in her throat. "Time?" The word felt hollow in her mouth, as if it had lost all meaning. Time had always felt so fluid to her, something she could shape, bend, and twist into whatever form she needed. But now, with the threads broken, the future seemed as uncertain as the space between the stars.

"Lyra," Aris said, pulling her gently toward him. "We don't have time in the way we once did. But we do have time to fight. We still have each other."

Her heart stuttered at the words, but the shadows of doubt loomed over her. How could they fight with nothing left to fight with? She had given up her voice—the very thing that had connected her to the world. Without it, what could she do? What could *they* do?

"Everything is collapsing," Lyra murmured, looking around at the crumbling stone walls, the firelight flickering in the distance, casting long shadows that seemed to stretch and writhe in the darkness. "This place is dying, Aris. The threads are breaking, the citadel is falling. We… we can't save it."

"No," he said firmly, his hand gripping hers, a fierce strength in his words. "We can't save the citadel. But we can stop the collapse. We can stop the Void from consuming us. From consuming you."

The Void. The name alone made Lyra's stomach churn. It was the consuming force, the one that existed outside the Weave, a darkness that threatened to unravel everything—the fate, the threads, everything that had ever been stitched together by the hands of the Weavers. She had always feared the Void, felt it gnawing at the edges of reality, even when she was a child, before she knew what it truly was.

And now, it was real. It was here.

The crumbling citadel was a casualty of its coming. The last remnants of a dying world, hanging by a thread.

She closed her eyes, the weight of everything pressing down on her, the emptiness filling her lungs. The silence had taken her voice, taken the song that had defined her existence, but she couldn't help but wonder if the price had been worth it. Was there still time to undo what had been done? Was there still time to stop the Void from devouring everything, from unraveling what remained of the world they had once known?

"I can't fight it," she whispered, her voice barely a breath. "Not without my song. Without my voice, what am I?"

"You are still you," Aris said, his voice soft but unyielding. "And you're not alone in this. You never have been."

His words cut through the fog in her mind, bringing clarity

in the most unexpected way. She had lost her voice, yes, but she hadn't lost herself. And Aris—Aris had made a choice. He had made a sacrifice, just as she had. His last remaining thread had been the one thing that could bind them, tie their fates together, and he had given it up to protect her.

It was more than she had ever asked for. More than she had ever imagined.

But it wasn't enough.

Not yet.

There was still a storm coming.

Lyra reached for his hand, pulling him toward the center of the room, the space between them shrinking with each step. They had no more time to waste. The Void was coming, and they would need every ounce of strength, every last thread of their connection to face it.

"We need to finish this," she said, her voice gaining strength as the resolve took root inside her. "We need to bind ourselves together, Aris. For real. The threads we have left—everything I have left—it's not enough. But together…" She paused, lifting her eyes to meet his, determination burning in her chest. "Together, we can stop it."

Aris looked at her, his eyes searching, weighing her words. He could see it in her—the strength that had always been there, the determination to fight, to survive, no matter what. But the cost of that fight, of what it would take to truly bind their fates, would be immense. He knew it. She knew it.

"Are you sure?" he asked, his voice low, a shadow of fear flickering in his eyes. "Once we do this, Lyra, we'll be bound. We'll be linked in a way that can never be undone. You'll lose… you'll lose the last of your voice, your magic. The power that you had before. There's no going back."

She hesitated, the weight of his words pressing against her chest. She had already given up so much. Her magic, her voice, her past, and now, here she was, standing on the edge of an abyss, ready to give up the last remnants of herself for a chance at survival.

But in that moment, as she looked into Aris's eyes, the same eyes that had once held so much pain and so much love, she knew.

There was no choice.

"I know," she whispered. "But I don't have a choice anymore. Neither do you."

The firelight flickered in the corner of the room, casting long shadows that reached out like fingers, clawing at the walls. Time was running out.

"Then let's do this," Aris said, his voice steady, his hand moving to hers. "Together."

They stood, hands clasped tightly, the last threads of their bond pulsing between them. Lyra closed her eyes and focused, letting the thread—what remained of it—flow between them. She felt it, the magic humming faintly, like the last note of a dying song.

Aris's pulse was steady, his hand warm against hers, but as their energy intertwined, she felt it—the bond that was more than just their connection. It was the final thread, the thread that would keep them together, even if it cost them everything.

The light around them dimmed, and as the final spell began to weave, the silence deepened.

And the world around them—the crumbling citadel, the approaching darkness, and the Void that waited to consume everything—faded into the black.

Together, they had sealed their fate.

Together, they had made the Songless Pact.
But the silence was no longer something to fear.
It was the beginning of a new song.

Eight

What the Moon Remembers

The wind howled across the broken landscape, a low, mournful cry that carried with it the promise of something ancient and unfinished. The moon hung high in the sky, its pale light spilling over the ruins like a memory, long faded but never forgotten. It cast jagged shadows across the land, stretching and distorting the remnants of the world around them.

Aris and Lyra had been walking for hours, moving quickly through the jagged terrain, the ruins of once-great cities now nothing more than crumbled stones, their history lost to time. But as the sky darkened and the temperature dropped, they found themselves drawn to the silhouette of an ancient observatory in the distance. The stone tower stood against the horizon, half-collapsed but still a testament to the stars and the constellations that had once guided the Weavers. Now, it was little more than a hushed ruin, a grave for knowledge that had long since faded from the world.

They approached cautiously, Lyra's steps quieter than usual, her breath shallow as she moved alongside him. The weight of the silence between them had grown heavier with each passing moment. They had walked through the night, escaping the collapsing citadel, the danger of the Void still hot on their heels, but there was something about the observatory that called to her. She had no words for it, but it felt like a place where the answers might lie.

As they crossed the threshold, the wind died down, leaving behind a heavy, unnatural stillness. The air inside the observatory was thick with dust and decay, the remnants of long-forgotten knowledge. Ancient maps covered the walls, their once-vibrant colors now dulled by time, their meanings lost to the ages. The telescope at the center of the room was broken, its lens shattered, its purpose abandoned. But Lyra could feel something else in the air—a faint pull, as if the stars themselves had once spoken here.

Aris stepped forward, his eyes scanning the room, the weight of the place pressing in on him. His hand rested lightly on the stone surface of the ancient desk, the faintest glimmer of gold flecking the cracked surface. There was something about this place. The very stones seemed to hum with an energy he hadn't felt in years. He could feel it deep in his chest, like a forgotten pulse, faint but undeniable.

Lyra stood by the broken telescope, her fingers grazing the remnants of the celestial charts. She turned her head toward him, her gaze soft, but her mind far away.

"We shouldn't be here," she said softly, almost to herself. "The stars don't speak anymore. Not for us."

Aris didn't answer at first. His eyes were drawn to the map

laid out before him—an astral chart unlike anything he had ever seen. The stars were not just mapped as they had been in the past, but woven together by intricate threads of silver light, each line a path leading from one point to another, each intersection a choice. The map was more than just a diagram of the heavens. It was a map of *fate*.

And Lyra's name was woven into the center.

He stepped closer, his fingers brushing the edge of the map, and his breath caught. The map wasn't just a chart of stars—it was *alive*. The lines moved, shifting slowly under his touch, a silent dance of light that hummed with energy. At the center, Lyra's name pulsed like a heartbeat, the light around it flickering as though it were something more than just ink on paper.

He could feel the pull of it. The power of it. The connection it held to her.

Lyra moved to his side, her presence like a shadow at his back, her breath soft against his neck. "What is it?" she asked, her voice distant.

Aris couldn't tear his eyes away. The map... it wasn't just an astral projection. It was a *weaving*. It was the story of their lives—of her life—written in the stars. The more he stared, the clearer it became. Her fate, her power, her *origin* were all here, in this forgotten observatory.

But there was something else. Something darker.

He stepped back, his hand trembling slightly as he traced the paths of the stars. There, in the lower corner of the map, was another thread—a thread that was tangled, broken, and dark. It wasn't just the mark of her origin, but of *his*.

Aris's chest tightened as he followed the thread, the feeling of guilt crashing over him like a storm. His eyes locked on the point where the two threads—the one that led to Lyra and the one that led to him—twisted together. He could see it now, the mark of his own betrayal etched into the very fabric of her fate.

Lyra's voice broke the silence. "What's wrong?"

Aris didn't answer at first. He couldn't. The weight of it pressed against him, suffocating him with the realization of what he had done. His sacrifice, his actions—he had broken something so deep within their fates that even the stars themselves had twisted in response. He had torn their worlds apart and, in doing so, had left her with nothing but the remnants of a life she could never fully remember.

"I've... I've done something terrible, Lyra," he said quietly, his voice hoarse with the truth. "I didn't just silence you. I *changed* you. I erased the very path that was meant for you. I broke you, Lyra."

Her gaze shifted to the map, her eyes narrowing as she studied the darkened thread that bound them. "You didn't do this. The stars—they—" She faltered, her hand trembling as she reached for the map. Her fingers brushed over the dark thread, the light flickering and dying at her touch. "This... this isn't just us, Aris. This is the world. This is fate itself."

Aris swallowed hard, stepping back. "But I was part of it. I chose it. I chose to break you—to protect you. I thought that by taking your voice, by taking your power, I could save you from the Weave. But now I see it. The stars—your fate—was never meant to be separated. And *I* did it. I tore us apart."

Lyra's eyes softened, but the hurt in her gaze remained, deep and unyielding. "I never asked you to protect me. You should have let me choose, Aris."

"I didn't know how to let you choose," he whispered, his

voice breaking under the weight of it all. "I didn't know how to let you see what the Weavers had already done to you. What they were going to do to *us*. But now I see. Now I understand what the threads have been trying to tell us all along."

She stepped closer to him, her hand reaching out to rest lightly on his chest. Her touch, light as a breath, sent a shiver through him. "We can't go back," she said softly. "We can only move forward."

Aris closed his eyes, his head bowing in defeat. "I've done too much damage, Lyra. The threads are unraveling. The Void is coming."

She didn't pull away. Instead, she stood there, her presence steady and unyielding as she met his gaze. "Then let's fix it. Together."

Her words were a balm, a salve to the wound he had carved into their lives. For a moment, the guilt, the weight of their shattered fates, seemed to lift from his shoulders, just enough for him to take a breath. He looked at her, really looked at her, and saw the girl who had once sung her way through the stars, the woman who had become so much more than the sum of their broken paths.

She was still here.

And with that knowledge, he stood a little straighter. "How?" he asked, the word barely escaping his lips.

Lyra's eyes flared with something like fire, something like life. She turned back to the map, her hand resting lightly on the silvered thread that now pulsed with an ethereal glow. "The stars don't lie," she said softly. "They remember."

Aris moved beside her, his breath shallow as he watched the path unfold before them. "The map… it's not just a guide, is it? It's a *record*. A story."

"A story of what was and what could be," Lyra murmured, her fingers tracing the thread that led to her name. "But it's also a path—a choice. And we've lost the choice somewhere along the way."

Aris looked at her, his mind racing, the pieces of the puzzle slowly coming together. "You're saying the map shows *our* fate. The path we should have walked."

"Yes," Lyra said, turning to him, her eyes fierce. "And if we can fix this, if we can walk the path the stars laid out for us, we might be able to undo the damage."

A tremor ran through Aris's chest. The stars had always been guides. But now, they were more than that. They were the answer.

The air around them seemed to shift as the room came alive with a faint hum, the walls vibrating with energy. Lyra's presence, her power, began to swell around them, and Aris felt it too—an awakening of something ancient, something that had been lost and now was beginning to stir once more.

He reached for her hand, their fingers brushing. "Together?" he asked, his voice rough with the weight of everything they had faced.

She looked at him, her eyes soft but resolute. "Together."

And in that moment, with the moon hanging above them, remembering the paths that had once been and the paths that could still be, they began to move.

The stars were their witnesses.

And they would fight to remember.

The room seemed to bend around them, the air growing thick with a palpable tension, like the moment before a storm breaks. The walls of the ancient observatory hummed, a low, ancient sound that vibrated through the stone, resonating with the pulse of the stars outside. Lyra could feel it, the faintest tremor beneath her skin, like the pulse of the very universe itself.

She stood there, her fingers still tracing the silken thread of fate that intertwined with the stars. The map beneath her fingers glowed faintly, its light pulsating with each beat of her heart. The threads, once disconnected and fraying, began to stitch themselves together in delicate patterns, weaving the fractured fabric of their destinies back into place.

But as the map shifted and the threads rearranged, Lyra felt something else. A tremor deep inside her, a rift that had never healed—a crack in the very core of her being.

"Aris," she whispered, her voice faint, her breath trembling. "I can feel it. The world… it's remembering."

He was standing behind her now, his presence like an anchor, the weight of his hand gentle on her shoulder. His voice was soft, steady. "What do you mean?"

"The stars—they're shifting," she said, her gaze fixed on the glowing thread beneath her fingertips. "Everything is trying to realign. The Weave… the threads we've pulled apart. They're calling to us."

Aris stepped closer, his eyes scanning the map, the dark circles beneath them deepening. The firelight flickered behind them, casting long shadows across the stone floor. He could feel the change too, a subtle shift in the air, like the weight of something impossible pressing against the walls of the observatory.

"The song," he said, his voice low, almost to himself. "It's *coming back*. But something's wrong. It's not—"

His words trailed off as the map shifted again, the constellation of Lyra's fate glowing brighter, its threads weaving faster now, the glow intensifying until it seemed to fill the entire room. The ancient observatory came alive, the walls trembling, as if the very stones could feel the movement of the stars. The pulsing glow cast strange shadows, distorting the lines of the map, and for a moment, Lyra's heart skipped.

"Aris… something's wrong." Her voice was tight with urgency, her fingers pulling away from the map, as if she were afraid of what it might reveal. "The stars—they're changing faster than I can keep up with."

Aris's breath caught. He stepped forward, reaching for her hand, but stopped short, his gaze locked on the shifting patterns of the map. "It's not just us, Lyra. It's everything. The threads… the Weave… it's unspooling."

The air around them crackled, thick with a dark, heavy energy, like the moment before a thunderstorm. It was the Void. He could feel it—its presence, looming just beyond the edge of the observatory, waiting. Watching. The threads were unraveling, and with every passing second, the world seemed to be slipping further and further from their control.

"No," Lyra whispered, her voice rising with panic. "No, we can't let it happen. I can't—I can't—"

Her words were cut off by a deafening crack that split the air.

The observatory shook violently, the ground beneath them trembling as if the building itself was alive and protesting its existence. Lyra staggered, her hand reaching for the desk to steady herself. Aris grabbed her wrist, pulling her toward him, his grip tight, fear flashing in his eyes.

"We have to finish this," he said, his voice sharp with urgency. "We have to bind it—*now*."

But Lyra shook her head, her eyes wild. "I can't. I can't give up any more of myself, Aris. I—"

"Lyra, listen to me," Aris interrupted, his voice breaking through her panic. "We don't have a choice. If we don't finish this, if we don't *bind* our fates together again, the Void will come, and it will swallow everything. The map… the stars—they can't realign unless we *seal* it."

His words rang in the air, cutting through the noise of the collapsing citadel, through the distant rumble of the Void drawing closer. Lyra felt the weight of it all pressing against her chest, suffocating her. But she couldn't breathe. The silence, the emptiness of the bond, the lack of her song—it was too much.

"I'm not enough," she whispered, her voice broken. "I've already given everything, Aris. What more can I give?"

He didn't answer right away. He only stood there, his hands trembling as he took her face in his palms, his eyes searching hers. His breath was shallow, his heart racing. "You are enough," he said softly, his voice raw. "You've always been enough. You just need to remember that."

Lyra closed her eyes, the tears welling up against her will. She could feel it—the absence of the song, the absence of her voice. The last piece of herself she had held onto was slipping away, and she wasn't sure if she could stand to lose it.

But she couldn't turn away from Aris.

She couldn't abandon him. She couldn't abandon the last thread that bound them together.

The map pulsed again, brighter now, as if urging her, urging them both. Lyra's fingers tightened around Aris's wrists, pulling him closer. Her eyes opened, and in that moment, she saw him—*really* saw him—for the first time since the bond had been severed.

She could feel his heartbeat against hers, the connection, the pull, the song she had once known so well, humming faintly beneath her skin. It was there. It was still there, in the space between them.

"We do this together," she whispered, her voice trembling. "We finish this… together."

Aris didn't speak. He only nodded, his gaze unwavering. He didn't question her decision. He didn't ask her if she was sure. He just reached for the threads, those fragile, fraying strands, and with a whispered prayer, began to weave.

The air grew heavy, the room filling with a low, vibrating hum, like the earth itself was singing. Lyra's chest tightened as the threads between them began to glow once more, the silver lines weaving and intertwining, binding their fates once again. But this time, the connection was different. This time, there was no song to guide them—only silence.

The thread between them grew taut, the energy building to an impossible pressure. Lyra's breath caught in her throat, her fingers curling into Aris's, as if she could hold on to something, anything, to anchor herself to reality. Her power was fading, slipping away into the ether, but something new was growing in its place. Something stronger, something more *real*.

Aris's voice broke through the silence, low and steady. "We're almost there, Lyra. Just a little longer."

But the words were a lie.

Because as the final thread of their bond wove together, a terrible, searing pain surged through her. It felt as if something deep inside her was being torn apart, ripped from the core of her being. Her chest tightened with a pressure she couldn't understand, and the room around them began to spin.

The Void was coming.

She could feel it, its tendrils reaching into the very fabric of the world.

"No," she gasped, her voice barely a whisper. "It's… it's too much, Aris. I can't—"

But before she could finish, the thread that bound them snapped, and with it, everything went dark.

The last thing Lyra felt before the world collapsed around them was Aris's voice—faint, distant—whispering her name.

And then, the silence returned.

The silence pressed down on Lyra like a weight too heavy to bear. She was drowning in it. The stars above her dimmed, their light flickering like a dying candle. The once-thrumming pulse of magic, the hum of the universe that had resonated through her very soul, was gone. The thread—her thread—had unraveled completely, severing her from the connection she had once had with the world, with herself, with Aris.

But she could still feel him.

His presence was there, not just in the air around her, but within her. Faint, fragile, a whisper against the quiet that had consumed everything. His voice, that last gasp of warmth, had reached her even as the void swallowed them both.

Her vision blurred as the darkness pressed in, and the pressure on her chest grew unbearable, until she could no longer distinguish between the weight of her own heart and the weight of the world falling apart. She tried to move, to reach for something—anything—but the ground beneath her felt far too distant, slipping through her fingers like sand.

The stars. The Weave. The song. It was all gone.

"Aris…" she whispered, her voice weak and hollow, like an echo that hadn't been spoken in centuries.

Her throat burned with the effort to speak, the effort to *be*. She wasn't sure if her eyes were even open anymore, or if she was trapped inside her own mind, the fragments of their fate swirling around her in a whirlpool of incomprehensible despair.

But then, just as the last vestiges of her connection to the world seemed to fade, something changed. A breath—his breath—reached her.

A faint, steady pulse of life—of *magic*.

Lyra's eyes flew open, but what she saw was not the observatory, not the broken walls and crumbling stones. No, the world before her was different. It was vast, and dark, and endless. A sky stretched out above her, filled with stars—not the stars she had known, but something else. Something ancient. A deep, empty darkness stretched before her, but the stars that flickered there were more alive than anything she had ever seen.

They whispered. They *sang*.

Lyra's heart ached as she reached out, her fingers trembling in the void. The constellations above her shifted, dancing in a language she hadn't known existed, but that she understood completely. It was a song of fate. It was her song. It was the *Weave*.

But something was wrong.

She could feel the pull of something else—the Void, the encroaching force that had already torn her from her past, from the magic that had once flowed so easily through her. The Void was coming, and it was devouring everything in its path. Even the stars themselves were fading, their light weakening, their songs dying.

And there, amidst the dark sea of stars, she saw it.

Aris.

He was standing just beyond her reach, his figure barely visible against the blackness, but his presence was undeniable. He was *there*, his silhouette outlined by the dim, fading light of the stars. His face was turned toward her, his eyes filled with the same sadness, the same determination, but he was farther away than he had ever been.

"Aris," she called, but her voice was drowned in the vastness of the darkness. She reached out, her hands grasping for him, but he remained out of her reach. He was slipping further away, like a dream that was fading before her eyes.

"No…" she whispered, a strangled sob escaping her chest. "No, I won't lose you. Not like this. I can't—"

The stars above her flickered, their light dimming further. The song that had once filled her soul began to die, its echoes fading into nothingness, leaving only the oppressive silence in its wake.

Lyra collapsed to her knees, her body trembling, her heart breaking. She could feel the weight of the silence crushing her, suffocating her, dragging her further into the void that was consuming everything. Her vision blurred, the stars dimming to mere pinpricks of light.

"I'm sorry," she whispered, her voice breaking. "I couldn't save us. I couldn't… keep you…"

But then, through the darkness, she felt it—a spark. A pulse. A thread, faint and flickering, but unmistakable. It was the thread they had both shared, the one that had connected them, the one that had been severed when she gave up her voice. It was *alive*. Faint, but alive.

Lyra's heart raced as she reached for it, her hands trembling as she grasped the thread that connected her to him. She could feel it, like a heartbeat, the pulse of their bond. It was a thread of fate, of love, of *everything* they had shared. And it was still there, still burning faintly in the darkness.

"No," she whispered again, more forcefully this time. "I won't lose you. Not again."

With every ounce of strength she had left, Lyra pulled at the thread, willing it to stretch, to reconnect, to bring Aris back to her. The world around her swirled in darkness, but the thread—her thread—was the only thing she could focus on. It was the only thing that mattered.

And then, as if responding to her will, the thread surged. It grew stronger, pulling her closer to Aris, the pull of their fates drawing them together once more.

Lyra's eyes snapped open.

She was back in the observatory, the cold stone beneath her hands. Her breath came in sharp gasps, and for a moment, she was disoriented, the darkness and the stars fading into the walls of the ruin. But the thread—the bond—was still there. The thread of fate had reconnected, and she could feel Aris beside her.

She looked up.

Aris was there.

His eyes were wide, his body tense, but there was no mistaking it. He was *here*. He was *with her*.

His hand reached for hers, his fingers brushing hers like a lifeline, a fragile, trembling touch. The moment their fingers connected, the thread pulsed, surging through them both, weaving their fates together again. There was no song, no magic, no words, but the connection was undeniable.

Lyra's breath hitched, and for a moment, everything stopped. The walls of the observatory, the ruins, the Void—all of it faded into the background, leaving only the feeling of Aris's hand in hers. He was still there. Still *with her*.

But the silence remained.

And the weight of the world, of the choice they had made, pressed down on them both. There was no more magic to bind them, no song to guide them. They had given everything to save each other, and in doing so, they had lost so much.

But they were still *together*.

And that was enough. For now.

But the journey was far from over.

The Void still waited.

And there was so much left to fight for.

Nine

Echoes in the Hollow Vale

T he Hollow Vale stretched out before them, a desolate expanse where the earth had turned brittle, and the sky was perpetually shrouded in an ethereal mist. The remnants of long-dead trees rose like forgotten sentinels, their twisted limbs reaching toward the sky, black and barren, as if they too had given up hope. The air was cold, but not the kind of cold that bit at the skin. It was a heavy cold—one that seeped into the bones and left an unsettling chill deep inside the soul.

Lyra shuddered as she walked beside Aris, her footsteps muffled by the soft, damp earth beneath her feet. There was something about this place, something ancient and wrong. A stillness that felt like the very pulse of the world had been stilled here, in this hollow, forsaken valley.

Her hand brushed against a rock as they passed, and for a moment, the briefest spark of memory flickered in her mind.

She paused, her heart skipping a beat, as the image danced on the edge of her consciousness, just out of reach. A violin. The sharp scent of smoke. Fire. A figure standing over the flames, watching as the music burned away.

"Lyra?" Aris's voice cut through the fog in her mind, pulling her back to the present.

She blinked, her breath caught in her chest. The memory was fleeting, like a wisp of smoke that slipped through her fingers. But the image of Aris standing over the fire, his expression unreadable, burned in her mind. What had happened? What was she forgetting?

"I—" she began, but the words caught in her throat. The memory was gone, replaced by the gnawing feeling that she had missed something important, something that connected her to him, and to herself.

Aris turned to her, his face filled with concern. "You're not well. We should find shelter before nightfall. This place..." He trailed off, looking around the Vale with a strange expression in his eyes, as though the land itself unsettled him.

"Not well?" Lyra echoed, the words feeling foreign to her. She was not well—was she? No, she had to be. She had the power to save them, to fix everything that had been broken. She *had* to be.

But still, the memory lingered. The violin, burning, and Aris standing over it. There was something hidden there, something her mind was reluctant to reveal. And in the deepest part of her, a whisper of doubt began to creep.

She glanced at him, her eyes searching his face for something, anything, that might explain the flicker of unease that had appeared there, just for a moment. Aris, the man who had saved her, who had sacrificed everything to bind their fates.

But the image of him over the fire, his face unreadable, gnawed at her.

Aris's eyes were focused ahead now, scanning the barren landscape, but she could see the muscles in his jaw tighten, the faint flicker of something unreadable in his gaze. She opened her mouth to ask him what was wrong, but the words died on her lips. The tension between them felt unbearable, as if something was shifting in the very air they breathed.

"You once had the power to sing fate," Aris said abruptly, his voice low and almost inaudible against the sound of the wind. His eyes remained fixed ahead, but there was a certain weight to his words. "I felt it the first time I touched you. The threads—the song that you held inside you. It was… *alive*. You were a Weaver."

Lyra froze at his words, her heart racing in her chest. A Weaver. *She* was a Weaver? The words didn't make sense, but they stirred something deep inside her, something she could almost feel, like a shadow brushing against her soul.

She had no memory of it. No recollection of ever wielding such power, of ever holding the song of fate in her hands. She had no memory of *being* a Weaver, but the way Aris spoke of it, with such certainty, it made her question everything she had thought she knew.

"How do you know that?" she asked, her voice trembling slightly despite herself.

Aris stopped walking and turned to face her, his expression shadowed, as if weighed down by something far heavier than the cold air. "I know because I *saw* it," he said softly. "When we first met, when you called the song, I felt the power radiating from you. It was raw, unrestrained. But then…" He paused, his brow furrowing in thought. "But then I saw what happened.

The moment I tried to protect you, the moment I silenced you..."

Lyra's breath caught in her throat. *Silenced*? He had *silenced* her?

"You… You took it from me?" she whispered, the horror of his words sinking deep into her chest. The doubt, the suspicion, that had been growing inside her now took root, growing heavier with every passing second.

Aris's face twisted with guilt, his hand reaching for her, but she took a step back. "Lyra," he began, his voice strained, as though the words were too painful to speak. "I had to. You were too powerful. The Weave—the threads—you couldn't control it. I thought I was protecting you. I thought I was saving you from the danger you didn't even know existed."

The coldness in her chest seemed to spread, curling around her heart. "*You* took it from me?" Her voice rose, louder now, filled with a fury that she hadn't known was in her. "*You* stole my voice? My power? *My song?*"

Aris's face paled, his lips pressed together in a tight line. "I never meant for it to be like this," he said, his voice a whisper. "I only wanted to keep you safe."

Lyra shook her head, the words catching in her throat. "Safe?" she repeated bitterly. "Safe from what? From *me*? From my own power? *From myself?*"

She turned away from him, her chest tight as the cold sank deeper into her bones. She couldn't breathe. Couldn't think. The very ground beneath her felt unstable, like the earth was shifting with each passing second, and with it, her understanding of everything she thought she knew about herself.

She had been silenced. And now, she was questioning

everything—every moment they had shared, every choice he had made for her, every thread that had bound their fates together.

The wind howled again, the trees groaning in response, and for a moment, the world seemed to tilt, the stars flickering above as if in answer to her questions. A violin. Burning. And Aris, standing over it. She could hear the sound of it—the final, screeching notes of a song dying in the flames.

"Aris," she said, her voice quiet, steady now, the fire of her anger burning out. "What did you do to me? What happened to my voice?"

Aris took a step toward her, his face full of regret. "You were too powerful, Lyra. The Weave—it's dangerous. I thought if I could take it from you, if I could protect you from the magic that was consuming you, it would keep you safe. But I was wrong. I see that now."

Lyra turned back to him, her eyes flashing with a fire that had not died. "You *muted* me," she whispered, her voice thick with the weight of the truth. "You took everything that made me *me*."

Aris opened his mouth to speak, but she held up her hand, silencing him. "No more lies, Aris," she said, her voice calm but firm. "I need the truth. I need to know what happened to me."

He stared at her for a long moment, his expression haunted, the weight of his own guilt pressing down on him. He knew she wouldn't let him off with half-answers, not anymore.

"I didn't mean to take it from you," he said finally, his voice tight with the weight of his own remorse. "But when the Weavers came for you—the moment they found you, when they realized what you were—it wasn't just your voice they wanted. It was *you*. They wanted your power. They wanted to use you. To control you."

Lyra's breath caught, her heart pounding in her chest. The Weavers. They had come for her.

"Why didn't you tell me?" she asked, her voice shaking now, not with anger, but with a deep, consuming sadness. "Why didn't you warn me, Aris?"

"Because I couldn't," he said, his voice breaking. "I was *afraid*. Afraid of what would happen if you knew. If you remembered what you were capable of. I was terrified of losing you, Lyra."

Lyra closed her eyes, the weight of his words pressing against her like a boulder. Everything—the pieces that had been missing—were starting to fit together. But with the clarity came a crushing realization.

The betrayal. The lies. The sacrifice.

The song.

Aris had silenced her—not to protect her, but to control her. To make sure she never became the person she was meant to be. To make sure she never remembered who she was.

And now, the pieces were falling into place. The truth was clear, but it felt like a thousand shards of glass piercing her heart.

She had been silenced. And Aris was the one who had done it.

The doubt, once a small whisper, was now a roar in her mind.

She didn't know who to trust anymore.

Lyra's hands trembled as she tried to steady herself against the overwhelming tide of emotions threatening to drown her. Every word Aris spoke struck like a hammer, driving deep into her chest, cracking the fragile understanding they had built. She felt cold, a chill deeper than the hollow winds that swept through the Vale. It was a cold that seeped into her soul, gnawing at her heart as the pieces of her past—of their shared history—began to collapse like a forgotten ruin.

Her chest tightened with the force of everything that was happening, the weight of the betrayal crushing the breath from her lungs. She turned her back to him, her feet moving before her mind had fully caught up. The hollow trees seemed to whisper as she moved between their gnarled branches, their leaves no longer green, but blackened and curled. They, too, had witnessed the unraveling of the world, the fading of magic, and they, too, seemed to mourn it.

She wanted to run, to escape the suffocating truth. But where would she go? The Veil was falling apart, the stars were dimming, and the threads of fate were unraveling. She was a broken thing—silenced, forgotten, and severed from the world she was meant to shape.

Aris's footsteps were behind her, hesitant, but persistent. He didn't know how to give her the space she craved, nor could he understand how much the silence of their bond suffocated her. He wanted to explain, to fix it, but the more he spoke, the more Lyra felt herself retreating. Each word, each attempt to explain, was like another cut to the fragile thread of trust they had left.

The ground beneath her feet was soft, the dirt cool and damp. Her fingers reached out to grasp the rough bark of one of the hollow trees, her nails scraping against its surface as if it could anchor her to this moment, to this world that seemed to be slipping away.

"Lyra, please," Aris's voice came from behind her, softer now, tinged with regret. "I never wanted to hurt you. You have to understand, I thought I was protecting you."

She laughed, a dry, bitter sound that echoed in the emptiness. Her voice, once so full of melody and strength, now felt foreign, weak in her own ears. "Protecting me?" she repeated, her voice trembling with something darker than anger. "From what? From *myself*? From the power that's mine to wield?"

"I was afraid," he said, his voice low, full of self-loathing. "I didn't know what to do with your power. I thought if I could silence it, if I could *contain* it, I could keep you safe from the Weavers, from the things they would do to you. I thought it was the only way."

The words sliced through her, sharper than she had expected. Lyra's fingers tightened on the tree, the bark digging into her skin as she tried to hold herself together.

"The Weavers," she murmured, the bitter taste of their name on her tongue. "The ones who would use me? The ones who wanted to make me *a tool*?" Her voice broke as she turned back to face him, her eyes burning with the weight of everything she was learning, everything she had lost. "And you—*you* silenced me to protect me from them? But you left me with nothing, Aris. Nothing but silence. Nothing but *emptiness*."

He flinched at the accusation, stepping toward her. "Lyra, please. I didn't know what else to do. I thought I was saving you from something worse. You were dangerous, Lyra. You still are. If the Weavers had gotten their hands on you—"

"I was never a *danger*," she interrupted, her voice growing stronger with each word, "until you made me one. You thought you knew better than me. You thought I was incapable of seeing what they wanted to do to me, incapable of protecting myself. You stole my power, Aris. You stole my *song*."

The tension between them crackled, thick and suffocating,

as Aris stepped forward again, but this time, his approach was slower, more measured. His face was full of something she couldn't quite name—remorse, yes, but also a deep, unspoken sorrow.

"I didn't know what else to do," he repeated, his voice softer now, pleading. "I couldn't lose you, Lyra. I couldn't stand the thought of them taking you from me. You meant everything to me. You *still* do."

Lyra closed her eyes, the cold wind tugging at her hair, her skin prickling with a sense of something familiar—something *lost*. The memory of the violin—the burning violin—flared again, this time sharper than before.

A flicker of a moment, of fire, of music dying in the flames. Of Aris, standing over it, watching. She could feel it now—the heat of the flames, the sharp scent of burning wood, the sense of finality. She had seen him do this, hadn't she? Hadn't she seen him standing over the destruction of something she loved?

She opened her eyes to find Aris standing just a few paces away, his face etched with pain. His hand reached out toward her, and for a fleeting moment, she almost took it. Almost.

But the doubt gnawed at her again. The image of him, standing over the flames, watching something precious burn. Her violin. Her power.

"Aris…" she whispered, her voice faltering, "Why did you do it?"

His eyes dropped to the ground, as though unable to meet her gaze. "I didn't want to lose you," he repeated, softer now. "The power you held was dangerous. I couldn't let them have you. So I did the only thing I could think of. I took it. I took it so they couldn't."

A shudder ran through her, not from the cold, but from the overwhelming realization that she had never truly understood the depth of his fear, nor had she fully realized what she had lost in the process.

She had no memory of the moment he had taken her voice, the moment the song had disappeared. But now, in the quiet of the Hollow Vale, it all seemed to click together. The pieces she had been searching for—about the power she once held, about the choices Aris had made for her, about the violin—had all led to this moment.

Her heart ached with a sharp, raw pain, and her mind swirled with questions that had no answers. Had Aris loved her, or had he only seen her as something to protect, something to control? Had he taken away her power because he feared what it might do to her? Or had he simply been afraid of the world that would consume her, and him, if she ever *truly* learned to wield it?

She took a step back, the weight of the truth heavy in her chest. "I need to know," she said, her voice barely above a whisper, "I need to know the whole truth, Aris. What did you really take from me? What was I supposed to become?"

Aris's eyes flickered with pain. He hesitated, as if struggling to find the words, but there was no turning back now. She needed the truth, no matter how much it hurt.

"You were the last Threadborn," he said quietly. "You were born with the power to sing fate itself, to shape the very Weave of the world. The Weavers—when they found out about you, they wanted to use you. But they didn't just want your voice, Lyra. They wanted your soul."

Her stomach twisted, and her hands clenched into fists. "They wanted to control me." Her voice was raw, the words sharp and jagged as they escaped her lips.

"Yes," he replied, voice barely audible. "And when I saw what was happening, I panicked. I did what I thought was necessary. I muted you. I thought that if I took the magic from you, if I took the song… they would have no reason to come after you. But I didn't know the cost. I didn't know that it would silence *everything*—including you."

The truth hit her like a tidal wave, and she staggered back, her breath catching in her throat. The pain of it was raw and unbearable. He had not only stolen her voice, her song—he had taken her identity, her birthright. The magic that had once been hers to command, that had been a part of her soul, was gone.

But it wasn't just that.

He had kept her in the dark.

He had chosen for her.

And she was left to wander in the silence of her own heart, a silence that had once been filled with the power to shape the world.

"I'm sorry," Aris said, his voice breaking as he reached out for her. "I was a fool, Lyra. But please, don't leave me now. I need you. I can't do this without you."

Lyra felt a rush of pain flood her chest, sharp and insistent, but she couldn't bring herself to look at him. She wanted to scream, to shout the truth at him, to let him know how much he had taken from her. But the words stuck in her throat.

Instead, she turned away, her mind a whirlwind of chaos. Her feet carried her across the Vale, through the twisted trees, and away from the man who had once been her anchor.

But she wasn't running from him.

She was running from herself.

From the truth.

From the world that had been ripped apart.

And from the song that would never again sing.

The wind whispered through the Vale, carrying the echoes of their past, of her lost power, and of the silence that followed them both.

And the stars overhead burned a little dimmer.

Ten

The Court of Silent Kings

The darkness swallowed her, thicker than the night, colder than the still air around her. Lyra's limbs were bound by chains of silver, cold and unforgiving, biting into her skin as she was dragged through the cavernous halls. The cold stone beneath her feet sent tremors up her spine with each step, reverberating with an eerie hum that rattled the air. Her head was spinning, her body aching, but the silence around her was the sharpest torment of all.

The Court of Silent Kings.

The name echoed through her mind like a ghost. She had heard the whispers of it, the legends that had fluttered like faded moths around the dark corners of the world, but she had never believed it. Not until now.

The Order had taken her, their hands cold and impersonal, like shadows that moved without a soul. They had bound her in chains that hummed with the weight of lost power, dragging her through the very bowels of the earth as the silence thickened around her, drowning her in its endless void. There were no words, no sounds but the scuff of their boots on the stone floor, and the unrelenting hum of the void that stretched out in all directions.

Lyra's heart pounded in her chest, the sound deafening in the quiet of the dark, but it was drowned by the deep, almost tangible silence that stretched into eternity. Her mind raced, swirling with confusion and dread. She had been brought here to the Court. To stand before them. Before the Silent Kings.

But why? What did they want with her?

Her throat ached with the emptiness. She hadn't sung since the moment Aris had taken her voice. She hadn't felt the pull of the Weave since. Her magic—the song of fate—had been severed, muted by the very hands that were supposed to protect her. She felt the echo of it deep in her bones, but it was weak. Faint. Hollow.

The Order stopped before a great set of iron doors, their dark figures silhouetted against the soft flickering light of distant torches. The door itself was an ancient thing, covered in intricate runes and symbols that seemed to shift as she stared at them, their meaning lost to time. They were imprinted with the seal of the Silent Kings, and Lyra shuddered.

"Enter," a voice, soft but with an authority that could not be denied, called from the shadows. The doors creaked open slowly, revealing the vast chamber beyond.

Lyra was shoved forward, her feet stumbling against the cold stone as she was propelled into the room. The air inside the chamber was thick with the scent of old wood and aged paper, a strange mix of forgotten knowledge and decay. The room was dimly lit, the walls lined with towering shelves of dusty books and forgotten scrolls, some half-burned, others simply withered by time. But it was not the shelves that held her attention. It was the throne.

At the center of the room, raised high on a dais, sat the Court. The Silent Kings. Three figures cloaked in shadow, their features obscured by dark hoods and the swirling mist that clung to their forms. They were still, motionless, like statues that had been carved into place long ago, their eyes never leaving her.

A chill ran through her, deeper than the cold of the room. She could feel the weight of their gazes—sharp, penetrating, ancient. They didn't speak, didn't move, but their presence filled the chamber with a suffocating pressure that made it hard to breathe.

Lyra's chest tightened. The air around her seemed to constrict with every passing moment, her heart thudding painfully against her ribcage.

"You have been brought before us, Threadborn," the voice spoke again, cold and regal. The sound echoed from the depths of the chamber, but it was impossible to pinpoint where it came from. The figure in the center raised a hand, and the torches around the room flared, casting harsh shadows across the stone walls. "You are the last of your kind."

Lyra opened her mouth to speak, to demand answers, but no sound came. She had forgotten how to speak—her voice was lost to her. The weight of the silence crushed her, making her feel smaller, weaker. She could feel the presence of the Silent Kings pressing against her, smothering her.

"The Weavers," the voice continued, "have long since faded. The song you once held in your chest was the last chord of fate. It was a power that could bend time, that could shape the very fabric of existence." There was a pause, and the air seemed to thicken with the weight of the words. "But that power was never meant to be held by one such as you."

Lyra's breath hitched in her throat. "What do you want from me?" she finally managed to croak, her voice ragged and weak, the sound of it foreign to her.

The Silent Kings did not respond immediately. Instead, they seemed to consider her with a cold, eternal gaze, as if she were a mere moment in time to be studied and observed. The seconds stretched into an eternity before the voice spoke again.

"You were born to sing the song of fate," the voice said. "But the song was too powerful. Too dangerous. And now, it is silenced."

Lyra's heart skipped a beat. The words hit her like a thunderclap, but they didn't make sense. She could feel the thread of her fate deep within her, faint but still there. The song was still alive within her, trapped, muted, but *alive*. How could they say it was silenced?

"*You* silenced it," she whispered, her voice sharp and accusing, her gaze burning with the need for answers. "Aris. He… he did it, didn't he?"

The Silent Kings remained silent, their forms still as statues, but Lyra could feel their awareness settle upon her like a weight, a burden that pressed down on her shoulders.

"You are correct," the voice spoke once more. "He *muted* you. And by doing so, he severed the very Weave that was meant to bind the world together."

Lyra recoiled, her stomach turning as the full weight of the truth slammed into her. She could barely comprehend it. *Aris* had done this to her? He had stolen her song, the last chord of fate, to protect her? To protect the world? To protect *himself*?

"The breaking of your song was not a matter of safety, Threadborn," the Silent King's voice continued, chilling in its finality. "It was the *only* way to stop the world from fracturing."

Lyra's mind spun. She had always believed that Aris had acted out of love, that he had tried to protect her from the Weavers, from the powers that would use her. But now she saw the cost of his actions—he had stolen her power, her identity, her voice, to keep the world from breaking, to keep the fate of the Weave from unraveling. He had silenced her—and by doing so, had sealed their fate.

"Why?" she asked, her voice trembling, her hands gripping the cold stone of the floor beneath her. "Why would you let him do that? Why would you let him silence me?"

"Because," the voice said, "the fate of the world was tied to your song. And Aris understood, as we did, that the moment you sang it, the Weave would shatter. Everything would be lost."

The words sent a shiver down her spine. "The Weave? The threads?"

"The threads of fate," the Silent King replied, "are delicate. If too many are pulled, too many threads torn, the world begins to fracture. Time itself loses its meaning. The Weavers knew this, and so did Aris. But in his attempt to protect you, to protect his love, he failed. He silenced you, and in doing so, stopped the fracture. The threads remained intact—at least for now."

Lyra's head spun. Everything she had known, everything she had believed, was falling apart in front of her eyes. The world was fractured. The threads of fate were broken. And Aris—the man she had trusted—had been the one to pull the final string, the one who had silenced her to stop the inevitable collapse.

"Why tell me this now?" she asked, her voice growing weaker with the weight of the truth. "Why bring me here, to the Court of Silent Kings, if it's all already done? If there's no way to fix it?"

The Silent Kings did not answer immediately. They simply watched her with cold, unblinking eyes, their presence looming like the shadow of death.

"You have a choice," the voice said at last. "You were meant to weave fate, Threadborn. You are the last of the Weavers, the last who can restore the song of fate before the world falls completely apart. The question is—will you accept it?"

Lyra's heart raced in her chest. Her mind screamed with a hundred questions, a hundred fears. Could she? Could she sing again, restore the Weave? Or was she doomed to live in the silence that Aris had left her in?

But more than that—*should* she?

She turned her gaze to Aris, who stood at the edge of the room, his face pale, his hands clenched at his sides. The weight of his betrayal crushed her chest, but she could still feel the remnants of the bond between them. There was love in him. She could see it in his eyes, despite the guilt, despite everything.

But the truth remained—he had *silenced* her.

And now, Lyra had to decide: Would she accept the song again, the power to weave fate, or would she leave it broken, just like her trust in the man who had once held her heart?

The world stood on the precipice of oblivion, and it all rested in her hands.

The Silent Kings were waiting.

The choice was hers.

And the silence, once again, was deafening.

Lyra stood in the heart of the Court, the weight of the truth pressing against her like a crushing force. The Silent Kings watched her, their hooded faces as implacable as the stone surrounding them. Their gaze was cold, yet there was something behind those eyes—something ancient, almost compassionate. The silence between them hung thick, each second stretching endlessly, suffocating her, leaving her no room to breathe, no room to think.

Aris stood at the edge of the room, his body rigid with tension, his eyes never leaving her. The space between them seemed to stretch, a chasm that neither of them could cross. She could still feel the echo of their bond, faint but undeniable. But now, after everything, the silence felt like a wall between them, one that had been built with years of unspoken words and unshed tears.

Her pulse was erratic, her body trembling with the weight of the decision that loomed before her. The Silent Kings had offered her a choice: to restore the Weave, to take up her place as the last Weaver, to sing the song of fate once more. But could she? Could she trust herself to wield that kind of power again? To undo the damage Aris had caused, to fix a world that had already fractured?

Lyra's thoughts spun, dizzying and endless. She had once held the song in her chest, a song that could shape the very world, that could bind the stars, weave the threads of fate. It had been her birthright, her magic, her gift. And now it was gone. It had been *taken* from her. But the Silent Kings said she was still the last of the Weavers, the last one who could restore the song before the world collapsed completely. The power was still there, dormant, waiting for her to claim it.

But could she trust herself with it? Could she trust Aris?

Her gaze flicked to him once more. His eyes were wide, his expression taut with guilt and desperation. She could see it now—he hadn't meant to hurt her. He hadn't meant to silence her, to take away the one thing that had made her who she was. He had been trying to protect her. But protect her from what? The Weavers? From herself?

She clenched her fists, her nails biting into her palms as the pain of the moment swelled within her. The man she loved, the man who had promised to stand by her, had been the one to sever the thread of fate that connected her to the world. He had chosen for her, taken from her the power that had once made her whole. And now she was standing before the very people who had known it all along—the Silent Kings who had watched over the Weave for eons, and who now expected her to be the one to save the world.

"Lyra," Aris's voice cracked through the stillness, breaking her thoughts. He took a hesitant step forward, his voice low but filled with the weight of his regret. "I—I never wanted this for you. I never wanted to silence you, to steal your power. But when I saw what the Weavers were capable of, when I saw what they wanted from you… I thought I could stop it. I thought I could protect you."

Lyra's throat tightened, but she forced herself to stay still, to hear him out. His words were laced with desperation, but they only twisted the knife deeper. She had trusted him. She had *loved* him. And yet, the truth of his actions—his betrayal—hung between them like a shadow that refused to fade.

The Silent Kings had given her the truth, the whole truth. They had shown her what Aris had done, what he had stolen. He had taken her voice to keep the Weavers from using her. He had silenced the last chord of fate to save her—*but* in doing so, he had condemned her to the silence that she now lived in. She could no longer hear the song. She could no longer feel the power that had once been so much a part of her. The threads of fate had unraveled.

And yet, here they stood—*together*, still alive, still breathing, but fractured.

"I never wanted to hurt you," Aris continued, his voice trembling now. "I thought I was doing what was best for you. What was best for *us*. But I see now, I see what I've done. I've taken everything from you. I've taken your magic, your voice, your choice. And I'm sorry. I am so sorry, Lyra."

The sincerity in his voice broke through the storm of emotions that raged inside her, and for a moment, the world felt still. The weight of his apology, the depth of his regret, was palpable, and it made the silence between them feel heavier, more suffocating. She wanted to believe him. She wanted to believe that he had done it all out of love. But the truth was, *he* had made the choice. *He* had stolen her power. And now, she had to decide what to do with it.

The Silent Kings were watching her, waiting.

Her gaze returned to them. She had come here to find answers, but now she stood at a crossroads. The future, her future, lay before her like a blank page, and yet the weight of the past seemed to blur it all. She could feel the song inside her, deep within her soul, faint but alive. It was still there, locked away, just beyond her reach. The Silent Kings had said it: *She was the last of the Weavers.* But what did that even mean now? She had lost so much, and yet the power was still there, waiting for her to reclaim it.

A deep, resonating voice cut through her thoughts. "The threads of fate are unraveled, Threadborn," one of the Silent

Kings spoke, his voice like the rumble of thunder, rich and heavy with an ancient authority. "The world stands on the edge of oblivion. Only you, the last of the Weavers, can mend the Weave. But you must choose, and your choice will determine the fate of all."

Lyra's chest constricted. "I don't know if I can." The words slipped out before she could stop them. The thought of taking up the mantle, of being the one to weave fate once again, felt like a burden too heavy to bear.

"You *must*," the voice urged, sharper now, as if the Silent King could feel the hesitation in her. "The Weave will collapse entirely, and all that you have known will be consumed by the Void, by the very silence you are struggling against. You are the last thread that can hold it all together. And yet, it is not only fate you will weave—it is *your* future, and his."

Her gaze flicked to Aris, whose expression was filled with a raw, desperate pleading. His hands were clenched into fists at his sides, and his eyes shimmered with unshed tears. He was waiting for her, waiting for her decision. And she realized—no matter what happened, no matter how broken they were—his future was bound to hers, just as hers was to his.

The Silent Kings continued, their voices a cold, unyielding command. "You will give the world back its song, or you will silence it forever."

The weight of the decision pressed down on her, filling her chest with an unbearable heaviness. She had been silenced, had been torn apart by the very man who now stood before her. But even through the guilt, even through the pain, Lyra knew one thing: Aris had never wanted this. He had never meant for her to lose her power, her voice. His fear had made him act, and in doing so, he had sealed their fates.

The silence—the emptiness that stretched between them—was suffocating, but it was not the end. She would not let it be.

She lifted her head, the weight of her decision heavy in her gaze. "I will do it," she said, her voice low but firm, steady with the force of resolve. "But I cannot do it alone."

Aris stepped forward, his face breaking with the intensity of his relief. "I'm with you. Always."

The Silent Kings watched, their forms unmoving, as Lyra stood tall, her hands trembling with the power that was stirring deep inside her, waiting to be reclaimed. She could feel it now—the song of fate, faint but undeniable, thrumming in her chest.

The world was on the edge of destruction, and only she could restore it.

And for the first time in so long, Lyra knew who she was.

The last of the Weavers. The last who could weave fate.

And it began with her choice.

The choice to remember.

Eleven

A Betrayer's Vow

The darkened halls of the Silent Kings' court felt like a tomb, the air thick with the weight of untold ages. Lyra's senses were numbed, the world around her little more than a hazy blur of stone and shadows. The silence pressed against her skin like a suffocating shroud, and yet, she could feel the hum of something deep within her, a thread of magic—of *life*—that pulsed faintly but persistently beneath the stillness. It was the only thing that kept her tethered to the world, to herself.

But Aris wasn't here. He had chosen to leave, to walk away, to make a sacrifice she could never truly understand. And now, even though she stood on the precipice of the most important decision of her life—whether to weave fate once again, whether to reclaim the song that had been silenced—she couldn't shake the image of him from her mind.

The betrayal. The silence. The choice he had made for her.

Her gaze flickered to the Silent Kings, who sat in their towering thrones, their hoods still shrouding their faces, their presence looming like an unyielding mountain. They had offered her the world, but the price was steep. The cost had been her voice, her power, and, in a way, her identity. But they had given her a choice—a single, fragile thread to hold onto.

She could save the world. She could heal the Weave. But first, she had to decide whether to forgive the man who had stolen everything from her.

"I will do it," she had said.

She would restore the song. She would reclaim the power that had been taken from her. But the path to redemption, for both her and Aris, was not yet clear.

The stone walls of the court echoed with silence, broken only by the soft shuffle of boots against the cold floor. The guards moved like phantoms, their eyes cold and unfeeling, their bodies built for obedience. But Lyra, standing before the Silent Kings, felt the tug of something deeper than obedience—something that burned like a distant flame, too far for her to reach.

The moment was stretched thin, like the finest thread pulled too tight. She had made her choice, but the tension in the air told her that this was far from over. Aris—*Aris*, the name burned in her thoughts—had walked away. He had chosen the silence. He had chosen to keep her safe by silencing her song, but in doing so, he had condemned them both to this endless void.

But now—now she felt something stir within her. The softest tug, a pull she couldn't quite place. It was as if the world itself were holding its breath.

And then, she felt it.

The air shifted with a subtle crack, and from the shadows, a figure emerged, his presence unmistakable, even before she could see him.

Aris.

His dark, unkempt hair hung loosely about his face, and his eyes—those eyes that had once held everything she had ever wanted—were filled with the same familiar fire. But they were not filled with hope. No. These were eyes that had seen too much. Eyes that had lived through more than anyone should. And yet, here he was, standing in the heart of the Court of Silent Kings.

His breath came in harsh pants as he stepped forward, the guards not daring to move, their hands resting lightly on the hilts of their swords. Lyra's breath caught in her throat. She hadn't expected this—hadn't expected him to risk everything for her, for the song that had once been hers, and for the promise of a future they could never have.

But here he was, risking everything in a place that had already claimed too much.

"Lyra," his voice rasped, barely a whisper, as if speaking too loudly might tear the fragile thread that kept him grounded. He stepped closer, his eyes fixed on her, his gaze pleading. "Please, listen to me. I couldn't leave you there. I couldn't let them take you, take us, without trying to make it right."

She stood still, her heart pounding in her chest as she felt the pull between them. The thread. The bond. It was still there. His voice, still carrying the remnants of the magic that had once been her guide, called to her. But her thoughts were cloudy, the anger—no, the betrayal—still fresh in her mind. How could she let him back in? How could she allow him to rewrite her fate when she had been nothing but a casualty in his own twisted version of protection?

Her throat felt raw, the absence of her voice—a voice that had once been capable of shaping the very fabric of fate—still haunting her. She wanted to scream, to shout at him, to demand answers. But the silence of her own body, the muting of her soul, held her captive.

Aris moved closer, his body tense but determined. "I know I don't deserve your forgiveness, Lyra. I know I broke you—I broke us. But I can't live with the silence anymore. I can't live with knowing what I did to you, to the world."

Lyra's fingers clenched into fists, the rage burning inside her like wildfire, but even through the fury, she could feel the thread stir once more—thin, fragile, but pulsing with the remnants of their bond. She wanted to feel it. She wanted to tear it apart. She wanted to scream at him for taking her magic, for taking her power, for taking her *voice*. But instead, she stood there, torn between the urge to run, to leave him and everything he represented behind, and the faint tug of the bond that remained.

"You think you can just *fix* this?" Her voice was raw, but she forced the words out, the sound rasping through her parched throat. "You think you can come here, after everything you've done, and *undo* it all? You stole my power, Aris. You took everything that I was. You *silenced* me."

The words were like daggers in the air, slicing through the silence between them. The rawness of her grief, the bitterness of her betrayal, filled the room, and she could see him flinch, his eyes momentarily clouding with guilt. But he didn't look away. He couldn't.

"I know," he whispered. "I know, and I can never take that back. But what I can do—what I *will* do—is this." He raised his hand, a strange glimmer of something in his eyes. "I'll make it right. I'll do whatever it takes to bring your song back, Lyra. No matter what it costs."

The air seemed to still as his words hung in the chamber, thick with the weight of their meaning. Lyra's heart stuttered in her chest. What did he mean? How could he—?

Before she could process the thought, Aris moved with a speed that caught her off guard. He knelt before her, his hands moving to the hem of his sleeve as he tore the fabric, exposing the skin beneath. The marks, the deep, jagged scars of someone who had fought, who had sacrificed more than anyone should, ran along his arm like a story carved into his flesh.

He turned his palm upward, blood already welling from the wound he had inflicted. He pressed his hand to the cold stone of the floor, the blood staining it red as he whispered, "I can't *bring* the song back by myself, Lyra. But my blood—*my sacrifice*—will restore it. It will bind us again. It will make you whole."

A heartbeat. Another.

And then the silence broke.

The moment Aris's blood touched the stone beneath her, the world shifted. The room seemed to pulse, to bend around her, and the quiet that had enveloped her entire being for so long shattered like glass. A rush of sound filled her ears, the quiet reverberating with the force of a thousand unsung songs, the music she had once known, the song of fate itself.

The threads stirred. Her thread—the one that had been severed—began to hum again, its faint pull vibrating through her chest, her arms, her fingertips. The power, the magic, *her song*, began to return, flowing through her veins like liquid fire. But as it surged, there was no comfort in it. No joy. No ease.

Instead, there was only a scream.

Her throat burned, the sound of it rising from deep within her, a raw, primal cry that echoed through the chamber. The sound was both agonizing and beautiful. It was the voice of someone who had been broken, someone who had been lost in the silence of their own soul. And yet, in that scream, in that pain, there was recognition.

His name.

"Aris."

The scream was filled with despair. She didn't know whether it was for the man she loved or for the life they could never have again, but it was a cry that came from deep within her—a cry of loss, of regret, and of the truth that no matter how much she had been silenced, no matter how much had been taken from her, there was one thing that would always remain: the bond between them.

The world held its breath, and Lyra, with the weight of her magic returning to her, could no longer hide from the truth. She had been betrayed, but she was still here. She still had the song. She still had the power to weave the world. And she still had the choice to make.

But for now, as the blood that Aris had spilled began to burn through her veins, she could only scream his name.

And it was the most painful, and yet the most *alive*, she had ever felt.

Lyra's scream echoed through the vast, cold chamber, reverberating off the walls like a sound too pure, too desperate, to be contained. The air around her crackled, a ripple of energy, as though the very fabric of reality had trembled in response to the force of her voice. Her breath was ragged, uneven, as her chest heaved with the aftershocks of the scream that had torn from her. The magic was surging through her, a torrent of power she had not felt in what seemed like a lifetime, yet it was tainted by the bitter taste of betrayal.

Her fingers curled into fists, the blood-red threads of fate weaving through her veins, but with it came a sense of *wrongness.* It was as though her own soul had been torn, stitched back together, and yet it was missing something vital. The power was there, flowing, but it was not the same. It was fractured—like a song that had been half-sung, left unfinished.

She could still feel him—Aris—his name reverberating in her mind, his presence still there, despite the rage that swirled within her. The agony in her chest, the gnawing pain in her throat, was the manifestation of the broken trust, the anger, the heartache. Yet, despite the scream, despite the confusion and fury, there was still the thread—weak, but *alive.*

And with it, the painful truth: he had *always* been the one to hold the thread between them, the one who had reached across the void to pull her from the edge of destruction. He had silenced her, yes. But he had also protected her, at a cost. A cost she wasn't sure she could ever repay, a debt she wasn't sure she wanted to.

Her chest tightened as she turned her head toward him. Aris was on his knees, blood dripping from the wound on his arm, staining the stone beneath them. His face was pale, his eyes wide, and there was a grim kind of resolve in his expression. He had *sacrificed* for her, but even in the face of her fury, even in the aftermath of her scream, his love was undeniable.

And it terrified her.

"Lyra," Aris whispered, his voice a raw plea as he crawled toward her, his movements shaky. He looked as though every ounce of strength had been drained from his body, but still, he reached for her, his hand trembling as it hovered just inches from her own. "Please. I couldn't let you—"

"You couldn't let me?" Lyra spat, her voice seething with venom as she stepped back, away from his outstretched hand. The threads of magic pulsed faintly around her, crackling with the same intensity as her emotions. "You couldn't let me *what*, Aris? Live? *Be?* I was never yours to silence! I was never yours to control!"

The air in the chamber seemed to thicken with the force of her words, the weight of everything she had been through, everything she had lost, bearing down on her. She could feel the fragments of the song inside her, each piece pulling her in a different direction, but none of them leading to peace. None of them leading to clarity. Just chaos.

Aris winced at her words, but his gaze never left hers. He was broken—his expression a mixture of sorrow and determination—and still, he didn't look away. He didn't back down.

"I never meant to control you," he said, his voice thick with the weight of his confession. "I just wanted to protect you. I wanted to keep you safe. You were the *last* of the Weavers. The Weave was breaking, Lyra. And if I didn't act, if I didn't stop the song… everything would have unraveled. And I would have lost you, too."

His words pierced her like shards of glass. The betrayal, the depth of his fear, and the twisted way he had *believed* he was saving her—all of it surged through her in a rush. The last chord of fate had been hers. Her song. And he had *muted* it. For fear. For love. For some misguided sense of protection.

But no matter how she tried to understand it, no matter how

she tried to reason with the past, the present *hurt*. And her heart ached with the weight of what had been stolen from her.

"*I* was never yours to protect, Aris!" she shouted, her voice echoing in the silence. "You made that decision for me! You took my choice! You took my voice!"

The words hung in the air, heavy, suffocating. But Aris's eyes didn't waver. The desperation in them only deepened, the pain in his expression raw and untamed.

"I know," he whispered, his voice breaking. "I know. And I'm sorry. But please, Lyra, don't let this silence be the end of us. Don't let the mistakes I made—my fear—define what happens next."

He reached for her again, this time with more certainty, his fingers trembling as they brushed against her hand, the contact sending a jolt of electricity through her. Her heart stuttered, the thread between them pulsing. Her power surged, but so did her anger, her grief.

"You think *I* can forget all of this?" she asked, her voice barely above a whisper now, thick with disbelief. Her hand pulled away from his, the thread of fate fluttering between them like a dying ember. "You think that after everything—after you *silenced* me—I can just forget?"

Aris closed his eyes, a single tear slipping down his cheek. It glistened in the dim light, a solitary testament to the guilt and love he felt. He leaned forward, his body trembling. "I know I don't deserve your forgiveness. But please… *please* don't let us break here."

The moment hung between them, thick with emotion, the broken pieces of their past scattered at their feet. The room was still, except for the faint hum of magic—Lyra's song, still there, pulsing beneath the surface of the silence. Aris's blood was still staining the stone floor, and yet, the thread between them seemed to grow stronger.

For a moment, the world felt like it was suspended in time—caught between the weight of everything that had happened and the possibility of what could come next. Lyra's breath came in shallow gasps as she tried to steady herself, the magic swirling in her chest, the power growing as her heart beat faster.

Aris was on the floor before her now, his head bowed, his hands pressing against the stone in silent apology. His voice, barely above a whisper, broke the quiet. "Please, Lyra. I'll do whatever it takes to fix it. Whatever it costs. But I can't fix it without you. You're the song. You're the thread that ties us all together. Without you… everything is lost."

Her heart hammered in her chest as the weight of his words settled in. She had been silenced, but in the silence, she had also been given a choice. And now, as the magic swirled in her veins, the world around her trembling with the possibility of everything she could reclaim, she knew that *he*—the man who had broken her, who had silenced her—was also the one who would help her find her voice again.

Her breath caught, her chest rising and falling rapidly, as she slowly turned to face him. "If I do this," she said, her voice barely a whisper, but filled with a quiet strength, "if I reclaim the song, we will be bound together. Forever. There will be no going back."

Aris's eyes lifted to hers, a flicker of something between fear and hope dancing in them. "I know. And I'm ready. I'll accept whatever comes, Lyra. I swear it."

For a long moment, the world around them felt like it was still, like the very air held its breath. Lyra's heart beat in time with the song inside her, the power growing stronger with each passing second. The threads of fate, her power, were within her reach. And yet, a piece of her hesitated. She had been silenced, broken, torn apart by the man who now stood before her.

But despite it all, the bond between them—*their* bond—was undeniable.

She had been lost in the silence, but now, she had the power to reclaim the song.

"Then we will face it together," Lyra said, her voice steady now, filled with a quiet resolve. "But you must swear to me, Aris. Swear to me that you will never silence me again. Swear to me that you will stand beside me, no matter what."

Aris's lips trembled, but there was no hesitation in his gaze. "I swear it, Lyra. I swear it on the threads that bind us."

And with that vow, the final thread of fate was woven.

The magic surged through her, the song rising from deep within her, louder and more powerful than it had ever been before. The room around them seemed to vibrate with the intensity of it, the stone beneath their feet trembling with the force of the magic they had unlocked together. Lyra's heart beat with the rhythm of the universe, the power of fate itself flooding through her.

And as the last chord of fate was struck, Lyra screamed once more.

But this time, it was not in despair. It was the cry of the world being reborn.

Twelve

The Unwoven Path

The Rift was not a place. It was a *feeling*.

Lyra could feel it in the air as soon as they crossed the threshold—a shifting, a rippling sensation that wasn't just in the world around them, but inside her as well. The ground beneath her feet seemed to ripple like water, and the air thickened as though it had absorbed the weight of a thousand forgotten memories. It was like walking through a veil of smoke, each step drawing them deeper into the space between spaces, where time and fate twisted into something unrecognizable.

She glanced at Aris, her heart racing. His eyes were wide, but there was a glint of something in them—something that hadn't been there before, something fragile and uncertain. It wasn't the same look of resolute determination he had worn since they had left the Silent Kings' court. This was something else. This was… doubt.

"Are you sure this is the way?" she asked, her voice a strained whisper, barely carrying over the humming of the Rift. The wind felt wrong here, as though it blew in every direction at once, shifting like smoke.

Aris hesitated, his gaze flickering to the horizon of the Rift—a horizon that stretched out, endless, bending and warping like the fabric of time itself. "It's the only way," he said, though his voice held the edge of uncertainty. "We don't have a choice. We need to find the thread. The song."

Lyra nodded, though doubt gnawed at her insides. The Rift was not just a place of escape—it was a space of choices. The path they walked here, this *path* they were on, was fragile, like walking on the edge of a blade. And within the Rift, there were no guarantees. It was a place where fate fractured and splintered into possibilities. Lives that could have been. Choices that could have been made differently. The very air hummed with the energy of those forgotten paths, of lives lived and lost, never fully realized.

Aris moved ahead, his steps careful but steady. Lyra followed closely, the tug of her own uncertainty pulling at her chest. Every corner they turned, every twisted path, seemed to stretch the very fabric of reality. And then, as they ventured deeper, something shifted.

The Rift seemed to breathe around them, pulling in the edges of time like a tapestry unraveling, and then it was as if the world froze. A ripple shot through the air, and before Lyra could process what was happening, she found herself standing in a different version of the Rift—one that looked impossibly familiar.

She blinked. The world around them shimmered, like a mirror cracking under pressure. The trees they had passed moments ago were now adorned with golden leaves, casting soft shadows over a clearing bathed in moonlight. But the eerie, fractured feeling remained. It was as though they had been transported to a memory that never truly existed.

"Lyra," Aris's voice snapped her from her reverie, his words sounding off, too distant, too fractured.

She turned to him, only to find a version of him she didn't quite recognize. The soft contours of his face were the same, but the way he looked at her—soft, affectionate, as if their past was a gentle whisper they could still hear—was not.

He reached for her hand, but this time, instead of hesitation, there was warmth in his touch. "This is it," he said softly, almost a breath. "We found it."

Lyra's breath caught. *This* was not the Rift she had known. This wasn't the fractured, twisted space they had entered to escape the Order. This was something else.

Something familiar.

Her heart pounded in her chest, as if it could tear her apart at any moment. She stepped back, trying to understand the impossibility of it. The Rift had shown them mirrors before, but this was too real. The emotions, the connection—this was the *life* she had *wanted*. The life she had dreamed of.

This was a life where she and Aris were married. Where they were not enemies, not separated by betrayal, not torn apart by silence. They were together, whole.

"Aris?" she breathed, her voice trembling.

He smiled, a soft, sad smile that she knew too well. But the words that followed were strange to her, unfamiliar. "I knew you'd be here. I've waited for this moment, Lyra. You and I, together again, the way we were meant to be."

A shiver ran through her. The words, the smile, the tone—it

felt like something *right*, yet deeply wrong. She had always imagined what life with Aris could have been. A life where they had never been torn apart by fate, by the choices they made. But this? This felt too much like a dream.

Her heart beat faster. She wanted to reach for him, to believe that this was real. But something inside her *knew* it wasn't. She knew, somewhere deep in her bones, that this wasn't her path. This wasn't the truth.

"Aris… this isn't… real," she whispered, even as the words tasted like poison in her mouth.

His hand fell away. His expression faltered, something dark passing through his eyes. "What do you mean? We're here, Lyra. Together. Isn't this what we always wanted?"

"No," she whispered again, the truth clicking into place. "No, this is just… this is a *what if*—a life we could have lived, but didn't." She shook her head, her pulse racing. "The Rift doesn't show us what is. It shows us *what could be*. It's not real."

The world around them flickered, like a fading star in the distance. Aris's form wavered, as though he were losing his shape, his color, his very presence, slipping between what was and what could have been.

"Lyra!" he called, his voice thick with a desperation she hadn't heard before. "Don't you see? We can be together here, forever. We don't have to go back. We don't have to face what we've lost. We can start over."

Her stomach churned. *This isn't real*, her mind screamed. The room was pressing in on her, the golden trees growing taller, the shadows deepening. The Rift was shifting, warping around them as Aris stepped closer, his eyes filled with longing.

But she saw it now. Behind his eyes, the lie was reflected—*this was not their path*. The weight of the choice she had made in the real world was still on her shoulders. It was still her decision to face.

As the world continued to twist, Lyra forced herself to turn away. She could hear his voice still calling out to her, begging her to stay, but she couldn't.

The world flickered again, and when she blinked, they were somewhere else. The trees were gone, the moonlight replaced by a crimson red that stained the air like blood. They were standing on a battlefield now, the ground cracked and charred, as though it had been scarred by centuries of war. The air smelled of burnt wood, the faint sting of rust.

And there, across from her, stood another version of Aris.

This Aris was different. His eyes were hollow, his features twisted with anger, his hand wrapped tightly around a blade dripping with blood. His eyes locked onto hers with an intensity that made her breath catch.

"I never wanted to do this, Lyra," the second Aris growled, his voice harsh and full of bitterness. "But you left me no choice. If we cannot have the song, then we *destroy* it."

Her heart hammered. *No*—this was wrong. This was a life they had never lived, one where their bond had shattered beyond repair. This version of Aris was consumed by the same darkness she had seen in the mirrors of their shattered trust. He was no longer the man who had protected her. He was the man who had lost everything—and had chosen destruction instead of salvation.

"No," she whispered again, her voice barely audible. "This isn't us. This can't be us."

But the Aris in front of her sneered, his eyes glinting with cold malice. "You don't understand, Lyra. If we cannot be whole, if we cannot sing the song—then there is nothing left for us but destruction. Nothing left for the world but to *burn.*"

Her hands shook as she backed away. This wasn't her future. This wasn't the path she would choose. The voice that had returned to her throat felt strained, but it was stronger now, more resolute.

She couldn't let herself be led down this road. She couldn't let the Rift choose for her.

As the mirrored Aris raised the blade to strike, she spun away, stepping backward from the battlefield, her heart slamming against her ribs. She couldn't do it. She couldn't live in this broken, twisted reflection of their lives.

But as she turned, the Rift shattered again, the world splintering into pieces, and with it, the choices they had made, the choices they had *not* made, the futures they had *could* have had. Everything began to dissolve.

Lyra's breath caught as she fought to ground herself. There was no escape from this mirror, no way to close her eyes to the versions of herself and Aris that had been, and would never be.

It was up to her. The path was unwoven—but she still had a choice to make.

The Rift trembled around them, and with a single, final breath, Lyra let it all fall away.

The future would not be written by the echoes of their mistakes. The song would not be lost to the past.

This was only the beginning.

The air crackled as the Rift stretched and snapped like a frayed thread, unraveling before her very eyes. It was as if the entire world around her was collapsing, folding in on itself, and the weight of every choice she had made, every path she had taken, was pressing in on her like a physical force. The mirrored versions of Aris, of herself—of the lives they could have lived, the ones they had almost taken—flickered and distorted in her mind, their echoes haunting her like a song that couldn't quite be remembered.

But the Rift was no longer just a place of reflections. It was a mirror to her very soul, showing her the broken parts she had tried so hard to bury. She couldn't run from it. She couldn't hide from the choices she had made. And the man who stood at the edge of it all—the real man, the one who had once been everything to her—was no longer a source of comfort.

Aris had been her protector, her savior, her betrayer. And now, standing at the threshold of everything they could have had, Lyra felt a fierce pulse of clarity surge through her chest. She knew, with a certainty that shook her to the core, that there was no going back. There was no simple path forward. The world had cracked in two, and she had to rebuild it from the ashes of the past.

The silence that had clung to her for so long still rang in her ears, but now it was different. She could feel her voice, the remnants of her song, stirring inside her—faint, like a distant memory of something long forgotten, but *alive* nonetheless.

"Aris," she whispered, her voice raw, a quiet plea hanging in the air between them. She hadn't expected to call to him, hadn't expected to reach out. But there he was, standing amidst the collapsing edges of their world, his figure barely holding its shape as the Rift continued to bleed time, fate, and shattered paths.

He turned to her at the sound of her voice, his face drawn, haunted. His dark eyes, filled with remorse and fear, locked onto hers. But there was something more in his gaze now— something she hadn't seen before: a deep yearning to heal, to undo the wrongs he had done.

"I'm here, Lyra," he said, his voice cracking under the weight of the word. It was the first time she had heard him say it with such rawness, with such need. He stepped closer, his movements slow, cautious, as though he feared that she might shatter under his touch. But Lyra wasn't afraid of him anymore. She wasn't afraid of the brokenness between them. What she feared was the silence—the one that threatened to steal her voice once more.

The Rift was starting to collapse around them. The twisted landscape, the fractured reflections of possible futures, were dissolving in on themselves. Time itself bent, snapped, and reformed in jagged fragments, like broken glass scattered across a shattered floor.

"Aris," she said again, this time louder, the words growing firmer in her throat. "We have to make a choice. We can't live in these reflections anymore. These *what-ifs*—they're not real. They never were."

His breath hitched, and he stepped forward, his hand outstretched toward her. "I know," he said, his voice low, almost a growl, "but it doesn't make it any easier, does it? To see what we *could* have had and know that we've lost it?"

"No," Lyra replied, shaking her head slowly. "It makes it harder, yes. But the truth is that *we've* never had that life. Not in this world. And we never will."

The Rift around them began to crack like ice, pieces of it splintering into nothingness. For a brief, surreal moment, everything seemed to hold still. The distant echoes of their mirrored lives faded, replaced with a deafening silence. Lyra's heart thundered in her chest, but she held her ground. This was it. The final decision. The moment where fate would no longer be a fractured reflection—it would be a choice they made together, or it would be lost forever.

Aris's hand was so close now, his fingertips just grazing her skin, sending a shock of electricity up her arm. But before she could take a step forward, before she could let herself reach out for him, something shifted. Something deeper, darker.

A sound.

A low hum, like the murmur of voices, rippled through the air. The Rift shook again, more violently this time, and the ground beneath them split open, cracking and rending, like the world itself was tearing apart. Lyra's breath caught as a figure stepped through the rift, its form outlined in the flickering glow of broken light.

The figure wore a cloak of black, its face obscured by shadows. A jagged scar ran down its throat, a mark of something ancient and powerful. The presence of the figure was suffocating—unnatural. It was a creature of the Rift, born from the very fractured essence of time and fate.

The figure's voice was a whisper, but it reverberated through the air, filling every corner of the collapsing Rift with a chilling finality.

"You cannot escape the path you've chosen," the figure said, its voice like the rasp of paper being torn. "The threads of fate have already unraveled. You are no longer a part of it."

Lyra's blood ran cold, but Aris's hand shot out, his grip tight around her wrist as he pulled her closer. "Who are you?" Aris demanded, his voice a low growl, but there was no mistaking the terror behind it. "What do you want from us?"

The figure tilted its head, and the shadows around its face deepened, obscuring any features that might have been there. "I am the one who holds the threads you have severed," it said, its voice filling their minds with an unsettling resonance. "I am the keeper of the path you have broken."

The air between them grew heavier, thick with an energy that Lyra could feel pressing down on her. The threads of fate—the *real* threads—were being ripped apart before her eyes. She could see it now: the Weave, once so vibrant and full of life, was unraveling at the seams, the colors bleeding into one another like a tapestry left out in the rain.

"You cannot bind it," the figure continued, stepping closer, its shadow stretching across the broken landscape. "Not anymore. Not after the choices you've made. The song is dead, and so is your future."

Lyra's heart faltered. She looked at Aris, who was holding her with a desperation that nearly broke her. His eyes met hers, filled with sorrow but also a defiant fire. He wasn't going to give up. He wouldn't let the Rift consume them, not without a fight.

"We can still fix it," he said, his voice low but filled with conviction. "We can still *choose* to live. We can't let this… thing take it all from us."

The figure's laughter was a cold, empty sound, like the chime of a bell tolling for something long lost. "*Live?*" it repeated, its voice dripping with scorn. "You are no longer a part of the Weave. You are *nothing*."

But in that moment, Lyra felt it—the faintest tremor, the whisper of a song, a pulse deep within her. She reached inside herself, feeling the threads that still remained, the ones that had always been a part of her, even when she couldn't hear them. And for the first time, she realized something profound: the Rift—the fractured world—was only a mirror of their mistakes. It was only a reflection of their choices.

And if she was going to save them, if she was going to save the world, *she* had to decide. *She* had to choose.

She turned to Aris, her hand shaking as it reached for his. And for the first time, she saw him—not as the man who had silenced her, not as the broken protector, but as someone she could *stand beside*, as someone whose fate was still entwined with hers, not as a shadow of the past, but as something *new*.

Together. Not fractured. Not broken.

"Aris," she whispered, her voice raw but steady. "We make our own fate. Together."

And as she spoke those words, the Rift trembled again. The figure before them hissed, its form beginning to dissolve as the threads of fate—the real ones—began to pulse with renewed life.

The world had been fractured. But they could still mend it.

Together, they would choose a new path.

And this time, they would walk it hand in hand.

Thirteen

The Void Sings Back

The silence was no longer just silence. It had become a presence. The absence of sound, once so pervasive and suffocating, had taken on an eerie quality, one that pressed in from all sides, warping the very air around them. It felt as though the world was holding its breath, waiting for something. Lyra could feel it deep within her chest—the Void, a dark, hollow space that had once been merely a backdrop to their existence, was stirring.

She stood at the edge of the crumbling cliffs of the Rift, the edges of reality torn and jagged, the landscape in a state of permanent flux. The world here seemed half-finished, like an unfinished painting, its edges blurry and undefined, where the Weave had once flowed in harmony. Now, there was only chaos. The threads of fate no longer weaved together. They hung loosely in the air, caught in a breeze that seemed to blow from every direction.

The ground beneath her feet shuddered, and Lyra staggered, catching herself on the fractured stone. It was as though the very earth was alive, shifting, twitching, as though it were trying to wake up, to *remember*. The wind whipped through her hair, a strange, biting cold that bit at her skin and rattled the bones of the earth.

It was in these moments—the quiet ones, the stillness—that Lyra had come to understand the full weight of what she had done. By singing the last note of fate, by reaching into the tangled threads of destiny, she had disturbed something ancient, something far darker than she could have ever imagined.

The Void was waking.

She could feel it in the very marrow of her bones, a pull like gravity, tugging at her, at the song inside her. It had been silent for so long—empty, void of purpose, a gaping maw of nothingness—but now, it was stretching, like a creature stirring after a long sleep. Something had changed. Something inside it had *learned* to sing.

Lyra's heart raced. The question that had lingered at the back of her mind for so long—the question of what had been disturbed, what had been set into motion the moment she opened herself to the song—was finally coming into focus.

She turned to Aris, her eyes wide with a mixture of fear and wonder. He stood beside her, his expression unreadable as he watched the horizon. His breath was visible in the cold, the fog of it swirling like ghosts in the air, and he seemed to feel it too—the weight of the change.

"What is happening?" she whispered, her voice trembling. She wanted to scream, to demand an answer, but the silence pressed in, as if the world itself were trying to keep the truth hidden. The world was breaking apart, but there was something—someone—beneath it all, pulling the strings.

Aris shook his head, his gaze still fixed on the horizon, as if searching for an answer in the blurred lines between the earth and sky. "I don't know," he said, his voice grim. "But I can feel it. The song… it's not just inside you. It's everywhere now. And it's *different*."

Lyra closed her eyes, and for a moment, she tried to feel it. To listen. The song—her song—had once been hers alone. It had been a thread, a whisper in the fabric of fate. But now, it had become something more. It was no longer just a piece of her. It was connected to the very fabric of the Rift, the space between fates, and it was beginning to resonate with something that was not quite right.

It was as if the silence, once so absolute, was now filled with a low hum—a vibration, barely perceptible at first, but growing louder with each passing second. The very air around her seemed to shudder as if something were awakening, stretching, hungry for the song she had once held.

Lyra's breath caught in her throat. The hum was growing, and with it, something began to stir inside her. The threads of fate—*her threads*—began to twitch, to pull, to move. She could feel the magic inside her, tangled, as it always had been, but now it was different. It was no longer a soft song of connection, of unity. Now, it felt *distorted*, like a song sung off-key.

And then, like a snap of lightning across a darkened sky, it *hit* her. The realization that had been lurking at the edge of her mind surged forward, crashing into her with the weight of inevitability.

The Void wasn't just an absence.

It was becoming *aware*.

Sentient.

And the more the Void *sang*, the more it pulled at the world, at the Weave, at the threads of fate that were fraying at the edges. Lyra could feel the pull inside her, the power, the need to release it. She could feel it in the deep, primal place of herself where the song had once thrived, a melody that had been silenced. But now, it was rising, not just as a call to herself, but as a call to the Void.

The Rift trembled again, and this time, the ground beneath them cracked. A jagged fissure split the earth, the void beneath it an abyss of nothingness, a gaping wound in the fabric of time. Lyra's heart pounded, and she took a step back, her hand instinctively reaching for Aris's arm.

"Aris, something's wrong," she said, her voice high and strained, the terror creeping up her spine. "The Void is… it's learning to *sing*."

Aris's face paled, his expression growing darker. "It was never supposed to," he said, his words more to himself than to her. "The Void… it's only meant to *consume*. It was always a reflection of what was lost, not a part of the Weave itself. If it's becoming sentient…" His voice trailed off, his thoughts racing faster than his words could follow.

Lyra could see the fear in his eyes now, the fear that had always been there, lurking beneath the surface. The Void wasn't just an emptiness—it was *alive*, hungry, and it was reaching for something. It was rewriting the world, twisting it, pulling at the very fabric of fate. And it had learned how to *sing*.

She closed her eyes again, shutting out the terrifying landscape that stretched before them. She could feel it now, the pull of the song inside her. It was begging to be released, to sing, to reach out to the world and *heal* it, to *bind* it. But she could also feel the danger. The threat. If she let it out, if she let the song run wild again, it could *awaken* the Void in ways that no one could predict.

"The Void will *consume* us," she whispered, her voice barely audible against the hum of the world around her. "And the song will… will end it. All of it."

A flash of realization struck Aris's face. His eyes widened as he turned to her, his expression stricken with something darker than fear. "Lyra… if you release the song… if it answers the Void's call…" He swallowed hard. "It could break the Weave completely. It could collapse everything."

Lyra shook her head, the weight of his words sinking deep into her chest. "We can't let that happen," she whispered. "I can't let it happen. But I can't stop it either. If the Void's learned to sing…"

The ground beneath them cracked again, louder this time, sending a shiver of fear through her. Something was coming, something was rising from the abyss below them, and she could feel it in the air—an oppressive force, a suffocating presence.

"It's *singing* back," Lyra murmured, her voice barely a breath. "The song isn't just inside me anymore. It's everywhere. It's awakening."

Aris's face hardened, his resolve settling in. "We *can't* let it. We can't let the Void rewrite fate. The song… it's ours to control, not to be consumed by the darkness."

Lyra reached out, grasping his arm, her fingers tight, her nails digging into his skin as she pulled him closer. "But what if I can't control it, Aris? What if it's too late?"

The Rift trembled again, more violently now. The ground beneath them cracked, splitting wide open as the song surged through her veins, echoing in every part of her. The air hummed with the magic, the very air itself trembling with the force of it.

Aris pulled her closer, his grip tight around her waist, his breath shallow against her ear. "We have to stop it together," he said, his voice fierce with determination. "You're the key, Lyra. You're the only one who can stop the Void. You're the *song.*"

For a moment, Lyra stood still, her heart pounding as she looked into his eyes—eyes filled with love, with fear, with hope. The song, the Void, Aris—they were all connected now. The choice was hers. The song could heal the world, could bind it back together, or it could destroy everything.

The Rift, the Void, and the threads of fate—all of it depended on her choice.

The air crackled as she closed her eyes, her heart in turmoil, and the hum of the song rising within her, louder now. *It was time.*

She took a deep breath, and then, with the weight of everything pressing on her, she made her choice.

With a single, aching cry, Lyra began to sing.

And as the first note escaped her lips, the world itself seemed to hold its breath.

The moment the first note escaped her lips, everything shattered. The world, the Rift, the very fabric of fate—all of it seemed to unravel in an instant. The sound of her voice, at first delicate and fragile, exploded outwards like a shockwave. It was as if she had opened a floodgate—no longer the soft hum of a single thread, but the roar of a thousand broken songs clashing together, overwhelming in its intensity.

Her breath caught as the energy surged through her, her

body trembling as if every part of her was being torn apart. She could feel the Void pulling at her, stretching out its tendrils like dark fingers, reaching for the very essence of her magic. It wanted to *consume* it—*consume her*—and Lyra fought against it, pushing harder against the oppressive weight. But the Void was learning, adapting, its song now merging with hers, distorting the harmony she had once known.

The song had been hers alone, a thread that wove fate, a pulse that bound the world. But now, as it flowed through her again, she could feel it slipping away, becoming something else—something darker. The Void wasn't simply listening to her; it was *responding*. It was *joining* her song, its voice rising with hers in a terrifying symphony that shattered the calm that had once reigned over the Weave.

"Lyra!" Aris's voice cut through the chaos, sharp and desperate. He was holding her tightly, his arms around her, his face pressed against her ear. She could feel his pulse, his heartbeat frantic against her skin. "Don't let it take you. Don't let it swallow you whole."

But his words were drowned out by the sound of the Void, its song growing louder, fiercer. It was everywhere now, creeping into the air, into the very ground beneath their feet. The Rift itself was collapsing, tearing apart, as the Void's song twisted and broke the very fabric of existence.

Lyra fought to keep control, to hold the song together, but with every breath she took, it grew more difficult. The Void was inside her now, its tendrils wrapped around her soul, and the song that had once been a force of creation was turning into something else—something destructive, something wild.

She felt herself slipping, as though the weight of the Void was too much for her to bear. The darkness threatened to overtake her, to swallow her whole. Her vision blurred, and she staggered, her knees buckling beneath her. Aris's grip tightened, pulling her back up, but she could feel the song slipping through her fingers.

"I can't stop it," she gasped, her voice barely audible over the roar of the Void. "It's too strong, Aris. I can't—"

"You can," Aris insisted, his voice fierce, unyielding. He pulled her closer, his hand gripping her chin, forcing her to look into his eyes. "You *are* the song, Lyra. You always have been. The Void is trying to control you, to rewrite fate. But you can't let it. You have the power to shape it, to turn it back."

She wanted to believe him. She *needed* to believe him. But the darkness was everywhere now, filling her thoughts, choking out the light. The weight of the Void was crushing her, its presence pressing down on her chest, suffocating her.

But then, something shifted. A flicker of light, barely visible, glowing at the edges of the storm of chaos that surrounded them. The song, the thread of fate—it was still there. Faint, fragile, but *alive*. The power was hers. The Void had learned to sing, yes, but it had not claimed the song. Not yet.

Her breath caught as she realized something. She was not alone in this. Aris was beside her. He had been with her through every choice, every moment. And now, as the song swirled between them, as the Void howled around them, she knew the truth. *Together*, they could stop this. Together, they could mend the Weave. Together, they could fight back the darkness.

"Aris," she whispered, her voice trembling but steady. "We can do this. We can fight it. *Together*."

The energy between them shifted. Aris's grip softened, his touch gentle, but it was a touch that was steady. He leaned in, pressing his forehead against hers. "We can't let the Void take it all. We can't let it destroy everything we've fought for."

The Void screamed, a sound like the rending of the heavens. It tried to swallow them both, but Lyra felt it—*her song*. The thread of fate, the very thing that bound the world, was *inside* her, woven into her soul. The Void could not take that. The song was not just a force of destruction. It was a force of creation, of *balance*.

She closed her eyes, focusing, reaching deep within herself. The song—the power—it surged up from the core of her being, pushing back against the Void, against the consuming darkness. The threads of fate had been fractured, yes, but they were not beyond repair. The Rift could still be healed. Time, fate, the Weave—they could still be *mended*.

With a single breath, Lyra reached into the depths of her soul, gathering every last bit of strength, every ounce of magic that remained. The song within her, the one she had silenced for so long, began to swell. It was not just a melody now. It was a *roar*, a storm of power that ripped through the Rift and shook the very foundation of reality.

"Now," she whispered, her voice strong. "Now we fight back."

Aris's eyes met hers, and for a moment, everything seemed to align. The Void, the song, the very fabric of fate—it was all connected, intertwined. And together, they could shape it. Together, they could rewrite it.

Lyra's hand shot forward, and as she did, the song burst from her in a wave of pure energy. It was as if the very fabric of time and space ripped open, the threads of fate weaving themselves back together with a strength and clarity that had not been there before. The Void recoiled, its song faltering, the darkness shrinking, as the light of the Weave surged through it.

For a brief, fleeting moment, Lyra felt everything—*everything*. The world, the threads of fate, the song that had once been hers. She was whole again. And for a single breath, she was no longer alone in the battle against the Void.

But it wasn't over. Not yet.

The Void was still there, still clawing at the edges of her mind, trying to twist the song to its will. It would not give up so easily.

"Aris, we have to finish this," Lyra gasped, her voice ragged from the strain. "We have to make the choice. Together."

Aris nodded, his face set in determination, his hands reaching for hers. As their fingers touched, the connection between them flared, a shockwave of power rippling outwards. The song of fate surged again, stronger this time, pushing back the darkness.

But the Rift was still shifting, still unraveling. They were not safe yet. They had only begun to fight.

"We can't stop," Aris said, his voice steady, his eyes locked onto hers. "We have to keep singing. We have to keep fighting."

Lyra nodded, her heart racing, her body trembling. But the song—*their song*—was growing stronger, becoming more powerful with every beat, every pulse. It was no longer just her fight. It was theirs.

The Void was breaking. Slowly. Piece by piece. And with every thread they wove back into place, with every note they sang, the world began to heal.

But the song was not without cost. The Rift still trembled, still threatened to consume them both. The song was the key— but it was a key that could unlock salvation or doom.

And Lyra knew, deep within her heart, that this was the moment where they would either save everything—or lose it

all.
The choice was theirs.
And the Void sang back.
The world would never be the same.

Fourteen

The Hollow Thread

The air was thick with the hum of magic, but it wasn't the comforting, familiar pulse Lyra had known before. This was something deeper, more unsettling, and as she stood at the edge of the broken stone cliff, watching the twisted landscape of the Rift collapse beneath her feet, it became clear. The weight in her chest, the pressure in her bones, wasn't from the Void. It was from something she had been running from all along.

The truth.

Aris stood beside her, but the distance between them was more than just the physical space. It was the gulf of unsaid things—the weight of a thousand broken promises, of words left unsaid, of a future that had been stolen from them both. The silence between them wasn't just the absence of sound. It was the *absence of trust*.

She could feel it now, growing like a shadow between them,

stretching out with every heartbeat, every passing second. The song—her song—had returned to her, but it felt *wrong*, jagged, like a broken thread pulled too tight. Every breath she took seemed to fracture the air around her, every word she spoke seemed to weigh more than it should. And through it all, she could feel Aris beside her, the familiar weight of his presence, the pull of the bond they shared, but something was shifting in him.

He was different.

No, not different. *Changed.*

And then, without warning, Aris's voice broke the stillness. His words were quiet, but they cut through the air like a blade, too sharp, too raw.

"Lyra," he began, his voice heavy with something that wasn't quite regret, but it was close. "I need to tell you something. Something I should have told you long ago."

Her heart stuttered, a cold hand gripping her chest. She wanted to say something—to ask what he meant, to demand the truth—but the words caught in her throat. She could feel the song stirring again, but it was pulling at her, tugging her in directions she didn't want to go. It was as if the truth would shatter everything, and she wasn't sure she was ready for that.

He turned to face her fully, his expression torn between something like guilt and something darker—something almost *resigned.*

"I severed your voice," he said, his words coming out in a rush, as though he had been holding them back for too long. "I did it because you were too powerful, Lyra. Your song—it was too dangerous."

Her mind went blank for a heartbeat. His words echoed in the silence between them, and then, with a clarity that cut through the fog of confusion, she understood.

She understood *why* he had done it.

Her breath caught in her throat, a bitter laugh escaping her lips before she could stop it. "You…" Her voice cracked, and she couldn't finish the sentence. There was no way to make sense of it. No way to make peace with it. She had trusted him, loved him, and now…

Now he was telling her that he had stolen the one thing that had made her who she was.

The silence stretched out again, unbearable, like the space between breaths. But this time, the weight was different. It wasn't the Void pressing in on her. It wasn't the song or the fractured threads of fate. It was the weight of his confession—the truth she had been afraid of.

She turned to face him, her eyes flashing with a raw fury she could barely control. "You *did* this to me?" she spat, her voice trembling. "You took my voice, my power, my *song*—because it was too *dangerous*?"

Aris flinched, the words landing between them with a crack that reverberated in the air. "It was," he said, his voice quieter now, tinged with regret. "Lyra, the song you sang… it wasn't just the song of fate. It was a song of *endings*. It was unraveling everything. Time itself, fate itself—it was *unmaking* the world. The Weavers knew it. The Silent Kings knew it. But they couldn't stop it. No one could. Except me."

His words struck her like a physical blow. She could feel them sink deep into her chest, the pressure of his confession suffocating her. He had *known*—*he had known* what the song had been doing to her, to the world, and he had chosen to *silence* it.

"No." Lyra shook her head violently, trying to make sense of it all. "No. You didn't—You didn't *understand*. You didn't give me a choice. You didn't *ask* me."

Aris's face was taut, his jaw clenched as though he were bracing for an impact. "I couldn't, Lyra. I couldn't *let you* choose. The song you sang… it was unraveling *everything*. You—*you*—were the Weaver of Endings. The last of the Thread-born, yes, but also the one who could destroy everything."

The words hung in the air between them, cold and jagged. Lyra staggered backward, her legs weak beneath her. The ground beneath her feet felt unstable, as though it were cracking apart with every step she took.

"Weavers of Endings," she repeated, the words tasting bitter in her mouth. "That's what I am? That's why you—*you*—silenced me? Because I was too dangerous? Because I could destroy the world?"

The idea settled on her like a weight, crushing the breath from her lungs. She could feel the song—*her* song—still pulsing beneath the surface, still trying to fight its way to the forefront of her mind. But now, it wasn't just a melody. It was a weapon. It was the power to reshape, to undo, to *end*.

"And I couldn't let you do that," Aris continued, his voice shaking now, his hands rising in desperation, as though he were reaching for her, trying to make her understand. "I didn't want to take it from you. But you were losing yourself, Lyra. The song—the power—you couldn't *contain* it. You were becoming something else, something that was tearing the world apart. You were becoming *more* than just a Weaver."

Lyra's chest tightened, a sharp pain shooting through her. Her voice trembled with the weight of the words she couldn't quite form, and the song inside her felt *wrong*, twisted into something dangerous, something *unholy*.

She could feel the magic surging again, growing stronger with every passing second. It was calling to her. But now, it felt like a poison—a temptation that could destroy everything. And with Aris's confession, with the truth he had finally spoken, she understood.

Her song wasn't just a melody of fate—it was the song of *endings*. She wasn't the savior. She was the harbinger.

"I—" She swallowed hard, trying to push past the tightness in her throat. "I never knew. I never knew what the song was doing. I never—"

"You couldn't know," Aris interrupted, his voice breaking, his hands falling to his sides. "The power was too much, Lyra. It was too strong for any one person to control. But you were never just a Threadborn. You were the *end* of all things. The Weaver of Endings. And I couldn't let that happen."

The realization hit her like a tidal wave. Aris had *done it to save her*. He had silenced her, not because he wanted to control her, but because he had believed, with all his heart, that her power was a threat—not just to him, but to everything they had ever known.

"But you didn't give me a choice," Lyra whispered. "You didn't *ask* me if I was ready. You didn't trust me. You didn't trust *us*."

"I didn't want you to *suffer*, Lyra," Aris said, his voice desperate now. "I couldn't let you destroy yourself. I couldn't let you destroy everything."

The song inside her flared again, the threads of fate twining together as the power surged through her veins, thick and chaotic. The pressure inside her head, her chest, was unbearable. She could feel the weight of the world—of fate—shifting, and it was all centered on her.

"I didn't want this," Aris continued, his voice broken. "But you are more powerful than I ever imagined. I didn't know how to stop you."

Lyra closed her eyes, trying to steady her breath, trying to push the confusion, the anger, the heartbreak aside. The world was falling apart, but she could still feel the song within her—stronger than ever before. It was calling to her, singing a song of endings and new beginnings, of choices yet to be made.

"I understand now," Lyra said softly, her voice steady despite the storm inside her. "I understand why you did it. But now, I have to decide what comes next. I have to choose what to do with the power you've given me back."

Aris didn't answer, but his eyes never left her. The tension between them was palpable, thick enough to cut through with a single breath. The air hummed with the weight of what she had to do—what they both had to do.

The song, the threads of fate, had always been hers. But now, the choice was hers to make.

And for the first time, Lyra understood what it meant to be the Weaver of Endings.

The choice would be hers—to heal or to destroy, to rewrite the world or to watch it crumble.

Chapter 14: The Hollow Thread *(continued)*

Lyra stood at the edge of everything, her chest tight with the weight of Aris's words. The Rift pulsed beneath her feet, its fractures groaning like the dying breaths of a world unraveling. The song that had once been hers to shape, to guide, was no longer just a melody. It was a tempest, a storm of possibilities, and in the center of it stood Lyra—no longer just a Threadborn, but the Weaver of Endings, the one whose magic had the power to destroy and create in equal measure.

The air felt thick with the tension between them, suffocating, as though every breath she took was another thread being pulled from the Weave. Aris stood just a few steps away, his eyes locked on her with that mix of desperation and hope that she had come to recognize in him. He had never been the one to tell her the truth—not until now, not until the very breaking point. She wanted to scream at him, to tear apart the distance that had grown between them, but she couldn't. She had no words left. Only the song. Only the power she had been given, and the terrifying realization that it was now hers to wield.

The Void had been singing back. The Rift was collapsing, and the song—*her* song—was the only thing that could save them. But the weight of Aris's confession hung between them like a shadow that threatened to consume them both. *She* was the one who could unmake fate. *She* was the one who could destroy it all.

"You're telling me," Lyra whispered, the words dragging from her throat like broken glass, "that all this time, I've been the one who could end everything?"

Aris didn't look away. His eyes were filled with regret, but beneath it, there was something deeper. Something darker. "Yes. You are the Weaver of Endings. The last of the Threadborn. Your song… it was meant to end the world. To destroy everything. That was your role—your *destiny*."

Her heart pounded against her ribs as she digested his words. She could feel the song stirring inside her, rising with each beat of her heart. It was so close now, so tangible, the magic a thick thread of power that connected her to the very fabric of reality itself. It was both terrifying and beautiful. But now, it felt like a knife in her hands, and she didn't know whether to hold it steady or let it fall.

"I never wanted that," she murmured, the words tasting bitter. "I never *asked* for this. To be the one who could destroy the world. How could you let me become that, Aris? How could you let me—"

"I didn't," he interrupted, his voice trembling now, his face etched with pain. "I never wanted you to become this. I never wanted to *steal* your voice. But I couldn't let you lose yourself to the power. You were too powerful, Lyra. You were starting to pull the threads apart. If I hadn't done it… the world would have been gone. Everything would have fallen apart."

His words were like a slap, but they didn't make the hurt go away. Lyra swallowed hard, the weight of his confession sinking deep into her chest. She could feel the storm inside her, the song rising, but there was no longer any clarity. There was only *confusion*. Her role had always been to weave fate, to guide it—but now? Now, she had become something else entirely. Something dangerous.

"Aris, you took it from me," she said, her voice trembling with the weight of the truth. "You took my choice. My power. You *silenced* me. How do you expect me to forgive you for that? How can I forgive you?"

Aris closed his eyes, a single tear slipping down his cheek, but he didn't answer. There were no words left that could undo what had been done. No words that could take away the years of silence, the power that had been stolen from her, the trust that had been broken. And yet, there was something in his eyes—a flicker of remorse, a spark of *hope*—that made her hesitate.

Could she forgive him?

The song stirred again, louder this time. It pulsed through

her veins, hot and burning, threatening to consume everything in its path. The world was shifting around her, the threads of fate tangling and pulling, ready to snap.

She clenched her fists, the magic surging in her, and then— *something* broke. A shuddering gasp escaped her lips as the power surged violently, threatening to tear her apart from the inside. She could feel it—*feel* the song, the threads, twisting and contorting within her.

"I—" Lyra choked out, her voice strained. "I can't control it, Aris. It's too much."

Aris stepped forward, his hand reaching for hers, his fingers trembling. "You *can* control it, Lyra. You have to. You have to control it, or it will destroy you."

She shook her head, her breath coming faster. "I don't want this! I don't want to be the one who ends everything. I don't want to destroy it all."

"You don't have to," Aris said, his voice low, almost a whisper. "You don't have to destroy anything. You are *not* just the Weaver of Endings. You are the Weaver of Beginnings too. You can choose, Lyra. You can rewrite it. You can make the world whole again. *Together*, we can do it."

Her heart twisted painfully at the words, at the hope in his voice. Could she really rewrite everything? Could she *choose* a different path? The song was rising inside her, a wild, chaotic force that threatened to pull her under, but something in Aris's words… *something* in him made her hesitate.

The Rift around them continued to tremble, the ground beneath their feet shifting violently, but in that moment, the world seemed to pause. Time stilled. The magic, the threads— everything seemed to hang suspended in the air. The Void had quieted, for now, but she could feel it—it was waiting.

Watching. And whatever she chose, the world would follow.

Lyra looked at Aris, her hand still trembling in his. His gaze was steady now, but there was an underlying current of fear in him, a fear of what she might decide, a fear of what they both knew was coming.

But there was also something else. A spark of hope. A belief that they could change the future, if only they could fight together. If only she could *forgive* him.

She took a deep breath, trying to center herself, to push aside the chaos of her emotions. The song, the magic—it was inside her. She could feel it now, vibrating in the air, like a thread that was hers to weave, hers to control.

"I can't do it alone," she whispered, her voice hoarse. "But if we do this together, Aris—if we rewrite fate *together*—we have to accept that it won't be easy. The world will *change*. We will change. And there will be no going back."

Aris nodded, his eyes never leaving hers. "I know. And I'm ready. I'll follow you, Lyra. No matter where the song takes us."

For the first time in what felt like forever, Lyra felt something shift inside her. The tension, the fear, the anger—they were still there, but they were no longer suffocating her. The song was still a wild force, but it no longer felt like a burden. It felt like *freedom*. The freedom to choose, to reshape, to create.

She closed her eyes, focusing on the song, feeling the threads of fate pulse with life once again. It was time. Time to rewrite the world. Time to reclaim her voice.

"Together," she whispered, more to herself than to him. "Together, we choose."

And with that, the song began anew. A new melody, not of endings, but of beginnings—of healing, of restoring. Lyra could feel the threads weaving around her, around them both, pulling the world back from the brink. The Void, once a dark and consuming force, was fading, receding into the distance, no longer a threat to the world they were going to rebuild.

The ground beneath them rumbled again, but this time, it wasn't a shudder of destruction. It was a pulse, a heartbeat—a new beginning.

The Rift began to mend.

The song, their song, was no longer one of endings. It was one of hope. Of possibility.

And as the first threads of fate wove themselves back into place, Lyra realized something. The future had never been about destiny. It had always been about *choice*.

And she had chosen to sing.

Together, they had chosen to rewrite fate.

Fifteen

The Price of Memory

The air in the clearing was thick with magic, suffused with the hum of power that seemed to seep into every stone, every blade of grass. Lyra stood at the center of it, her heart pounding, her breath shallow as she stared at Aris, whose figure loomed before her, his expression grim but resolute. The winds whispered around them, carrying the heavy weight of what was to come.

The song inside her was stronger now, louder than it had ever been. It vibrated within her chest, humming in her veins, filling every part of her. It was a force of creation, of rebuilding. A melody that could heal or destroy—something that could rewrite fate itself. She could feel it pulsing through her, ready to be unleashed.

But there was a price.

"You must give something to the song," the figure—the entity that had guided them this far—had said. The voice had come from nowhere and everywhere, a resonance of ancient power. It had been a warning, an inevitability: *To unlock the full song, to heal the Weave and restore the world, Lyra must sacrifice something precious. The price of memory.*

She had hoped it wasn't true. She had prayed that she wouldn't have to pay that price—that she wouldn't have to sacrifice the most important thing in her life. But standing here, with the song pounding in her ears, with the weight of Aris's gaze on her, Lyra understood. She knew the truth, even if it was more terrifying than she could bear.

The price of the song was her memory.

Her *memory of him.*

She swallowed hard, the words stuck in her throat. She wanted to scream, to argue, to run far, far away from this reality. But the threads of fate around her pulsed in rhythm with the song—unyielding, binding, and the song would not wait.

Aris stepped forward, his eyes locked on hers, his face as solemn as a man stepping toward his death. His lips were pressed tightly together, the strain of the decision clear in the lines of his jaw. He had made his choice. He always did, didn't he?

"I'll do it," Aris said, his voice soft but resolute. "I'll give up my memory of you. If you won't sacrifice yours, then I'll sacrifice mine."

Lyra's breath hitched in her throat, her body recoiling as though she had been struck. "No." Her voice was sharp, fierce. "You don't *get* to make that decision for me. You don't *get* to give up your memories for mine."

"But I will," he said, stepping closer still. His hands were trembling at his sides, his eyes clouded with the weight of his offer. "I've always known this was the price. I can't stand to see you lose yourself—if it's me that you have to forget, then let it be. I'll bear it, I'll carry the burden if it means you can have everything else."

Lyra's heart cracked in her chest. The song, powerful and overwhelming, swirled through her, and she could feel the weight of his sacrifice, the depth of his love. The tenderness, the tenderness that had once bound them so completely, was still there. But now, the choice—his choice—felt like a wedge being driven between them.

"No," Lyra whispered again, her voice breaking. "*No*, Aris. You can't. I won't let you."

The song inside her surged, a fierce tide that threatened to overwhelm everything. The ground beneath their feet trembled, as if the earth itself understood the weight of what they were facing. The air became heavier, thick with the tension of the choice they both had to make.

Aris was still standing there, his eyes locked on hers, his expression pained but firm. The time was slipping away. They both knew it. The song—the Weave—was waiting for them to act.

"You'll forget me, Lyra," Aris said, his voice soft now, tender, as if he were speaking to a part of her that had already gone. "If you don't give up your memory, if you don't let it go… then I'll be nothing. You won't remember me. You won't remember *us*. You'll lose everything, and I can't bear that. Not after everything we've been through. Not after everything we could still be."

Lyra's eyes filled with tears, and she turned away from him, her hands pressed to her temples as the weight of his words pressed down on her like a stone. She *couldn't* let him do this. She *couldn't* let him take on this sacrifice, this cost. He was already giving so much. But the idea of him, of Aris, disappearing from her life—*forgetting her*, forgetting them— was a pain that cut deeper than any wound she had ever known.

"I won't forget you," she whispered, her voice thick with tears. "I can't. I won't let the song steal you from me. I won't *lose* you again."

But the truth was unbearable. She knew, deep in her bones, that the price of unlocking the song, of saving the Weave, of healing the world, was too great. She couldn't have it all. Not the way she wanted. She couldn't have the world *and* Aris.

Her chest tightened as she felt the song rise, the power surging through her, louder now, and it was almost too much to bear. The threads were unraveling in her mind, the memories slipping away like sand through her fingers. The path was clear. She could feel it, the sacrifice she had to make.

"You don't have to do this for me," Lyra said, turning to face him again, her voice breaking with the weight of her decision. She couldn't look at him for too long. His face was so full of love, of the burden he was carrying, and it was breaking her. "You can't give up your memory for me, Aris. I won't let you."

Aris stepped forward again, his hand reaching out toward her, as though he was trying to bridge the distance between their hearts. His fingers trembled as they brushed against her cheek. "You don't have a choice, Lyra. This is the price. I know it. I'm willing to lose myself for you, for us. It's the only way."

"No," Lyra whispered, taking a step back, shaking her head, her mind racing. "I *won't* let you. I *refuse*."

The song surged again, fiercer this time, like a storm break- ing over the horizon. The pressure in the air grew unbearable, the weight of their choices pressing against her chest, and yet

Lyra could feel something—*something new*—rising within her.

She could feel the power, the song of endings and beginnings, but there was another thread in her—a thread of something different. A choice, a realization, one she had never made before, not like this.

With a deep breath, Lyra reached out to him, her hand trembling as it touched his. She looked into his eyes, her voice steady despite the turmoil inside her. "We will *both* remember. We will *both* carry the burden. Not just me. Not just you. Together."

Aris froze, his breath caught in his throat as he stared at her, confusion flashing across his face. "But you… you'll lose everything. You won't remember—"

"No," she interrupted, shaking her head firmly. "We don't need to forget to heal. We can't rewrite fate, Aris, but we can choose to bear it *together*. I won't let you make this sacrifice alone. I won't let you *lose* yourself for me."

Her fingers tightened around his, the threads of fate pulsing between them. The song swelled once more, louder than before, but this time it was different. It was no longer the song of endings, but the song of shared loss. The song of *togetherness*.

"I'm ready," Lyra said, her voice trembling, but full of conviction. "Together."

The ground beneath them trembled once more, the weight of their choice shifting the very air around them. The Rift had begun to collapse again, but this time, the shift wasn't one of destruction. It was one of change, of creation.

With a single breath, Lyra and Aris reached out together, and the song—*their song*—was woven between them. It was not just a melody. It was a promise.

A song of shared loss.

A song of *love*.

And as they stood together, bound in that song, the world around them began to change. The Rift shifted, its edges blurring into the horizon, and the magic surged between them, binding their fates once more.

The Weave would heal, and the world would move forward—*together*.

But the price of memory had been paid. And nothing would ever be the same again.

The song wrapped around them both, binding their fates like threads woven into an intricate tapestry—complex and delicate, fragile and eternal. Lyra felt it surge through her, a magic so ancient and pure, like the first thread of creation. She could feel the pulse of the Weave growing stronger, but it was more than just the threads of fate. It was her power. Their power. The song of beginnings and endings, of love and loss.

And yet, with the magic came a price.

Lyra's heart ached as the power swelled within her. The world was shifting, bending to the will of the song, but the weight of their decision pressed down on her chest. She could feel the memories—slipping away. Aris, his face, the moments they had shared, the love that had once bound them together—they were all fading, like wisps of smoke in a storm.

She could sense the space between them growing, the thread of their connection unraveling, not by their choice, but by the force of the song. She felt it as much as she *saw* it—like an invisible chain stretching, pulling them apart. Each breath she took, each moment she lingered in the bond they shared, seemed to take away a little more of their past.

But she couldn't stop it. She wouldn't.

She *wouldn't* let him forget. *Not yet.*

The air was thick with magic, and yet, beneath it all, Lyra could feel the empty ache, the loss that she had agreed to. It was a wound in her soul, a painful realization that she was losing something precious, something irreplaceable. Memories were not just fragments of the past. They were *who* they were—who they had been. They were the truth of their connection. But they were slipping away.

Lyra's breath was shaky as she reached for Aris, her fingers trembling as they brushed against his arm. She knew that every touch, every moment she shared with him now, was precious. She could feel the thread of their bond tugging at her, weaker now, but still there, still *alive*.

His eyes met hers, his expression unreadable, but Lyra could feel the weight of his love in his gaze. He hadn't wanted this. He hadn't wanted her to sacrifice her memories for the song. And yet, in the depths of her heart, she could see it now—he had wanted her to remember. He had wanted her to keep her *choice*. To be whole.

But the song was a force beyond them.

"I won't forget you," she whispered, her voice breaking. "I won't forget us. I can't. But… it's slipping. It's slipping away, Aris. I can't hold on to it."

Aris's face softened with sorrow, and he gently cupped her cheek, his thumb brushing the line of her jaw. "Lyra, you'll never truly forget," he murmured, his voice filled with quiet desperation. "No matter what the song takes, no matter what you lose… you'll never forget *this*."

He leaned in, his lips brushing against her forehead. Lyra could feel his heartbeat against her, a steady rhythm that seemed to anchor her in the storm of the magic. She closed her eyes, leaning into him, desperate to hold on to this moment, to the way it felt to be with him. To the way it had always felt.

And yet, she could feel it—the pull of the song, the twisting of the threads, the sharp sting of the price she had paid. Her memories, like shards of glass, were slipping between her fingers, and there was nothing she could do to stop it.

Aris's voice broke through the haze in her mind, soft but insistent. "If we're going to move forward, if we're going to rebuild the world—*together*—we have to let go of the past."

Her eyes snapped open, her heart thudding in her chest. "But you're part of my past, Aris. You're part of everything I've ever known. I can't—"

"You *can*, Lyra," he interrupted gently, his hand moving from her cheek to her shoulder, squeezing it as if trying to hold her together. "You can move forward with me. The memories we've made together will never truly leave you. They're *part* of you, no matter what happens. But if we're going to be whole again, we can't live in the past. We can't keep trying to hold on to what's already slipping away."

She shook her head, a bitter laugh escaping her lips as the tears threatened to fall. "It's not that simple, Aris. How do you let go of something you've loved? How do you let go of someone you've *been*?"

Aris took a deep breath, the weight of his words heavy in the air. "I don't know. But what I do know is that we have the chance to make something new. To rebuild. To heal. To rewrite the song of fate *together*."

The song inside her pulsed again, the threads of fate vibrating with energy, and Lyra's vision blurred as the magic surged within her. She could feel it pulling at her, tugging at her memories, at everything she had ever known. The song was rising, demanding to be released, demanding her *sacrifice*. She could feel Aris's presence beside her, the bond between them flickering, but the connection was fading. The sacrifice was happening—slowly, steadily, but it was happening.

And then, something deep within her heart clicked. It was not a clear thought, not a conscious decision, but a realization— a choice she had been too afraid to make. The song had always been about endings, about the destruction of what was. But what if… what if she could take that power and shape it into something new? What if she could *remake* the Weave without sacrificing the love that had brought her here?

The song surged within her, louder than before, as though it was answering her unspoken question.

"Aris," she said, her voice steady now, filled with a quiet resolution. "I will not forget you. I will not let go of what we have—what we *are*. But I won't give in to the darkness of the song. Not anymore. I will take it, yes. I will take the threads of fate. But I will not let them break me. I won't let them *break* us."

Aris's eyes flickered with something that could have been hope—or fear—and then, slowly, he nodded. "We will rebuild it, Lyra. Together."

With a deep breath, Lyra reached for the song. Her fingers trembled, but she was no longer afraid of it. The threads of fate that had once seemed like a curse now felt like an opportunity— an opportunity to shape something better. She would not let the song destroy everything. She would rewrite it. Reweave it.

And, in doing so, she would keep Aris in her heart.

The power surged through her, a force so great that it threatened to shatter the very air around them. The world seemed to tremble in response, the magic pulling at the edges of reality, reshaping everything.

The song—her song—was no longer the end. It was the beginning.

And with that final realization, the threads of fate began to shift. They rewove, together. And though the cost had been high, the price of memory paid, Lyra felt the spark of something new—something *alive*.

Together, they had made it.

And together, they would rebuild the world.

Sixteen

The Breath Between Notes

The world stretched before them, endless and beautiful, yet suffocating. Lyra felt it in her chest, the tension in the air as they approached the First Loom. She could see its silhouette in the distance—a towering structure, ancient and humming with power, its machinery wrapped in the threads of fate. It was said to be the heart of all creation, where the Weavers once wove the fabric of the world itself. Now, it stood like a forgotten monument to a lost age, covered in the dust of centuries and the weight of memories.

Beside her, Aris moved silently, his presence like a shadow that clung to her even in the most dangerous of times. She could feel the bond between them, deepening with each step they took. The threads of fate had been reforged, but it felt as though something more had been woven between them— a connection that was beyond magic, beyond song. It was something far older. A destiny they could no longer deny.

Her hand brushed against his, and for a moment, everything slowed. The air was thick with the scent of rain and earth, the remnants of a storm that had passed through the valley just hours before. The scent clung to the atmosphere, fresh and heavy, grounding them both in a world that felt as though it were on the verge of slipping into something else entirely.

"I can feel it, Aris," Lyra whispered, her voice soft but trembling with an unspoken fear. "The Loom… It's calling to us. But something's wrong."

Aris glanced down at her, his jaw set in a way that spoke of resolve, but his eyes flickered with uncertainty. "The Loom is the only chance we have left to fix this—to rewrite fate. We can undo the damage that's been done."

But as Lyra looked ahead, she could see the way the Loom towered before them like a beast—silent, ominous, its once-great wheels now still, its vast, skeletal structure wrapped in dark energy. There was no hum of life, no song vibrating through its core. It was silent, as though it had been abandoned by time itself. And in the silence, Lyra could feel it—the presence of something else, something far older and more dangerous, stirring deep in the heart of the Loom.

The Void.

Her pulse quickened at the thought. She had felt it, too. The pull, the faint tug of darkness that seemed to throb in rhythm with the beating of her heart. She could feel it in the edges of the world around them, where the air grew cold and the light began to fade.

"The Void has already reached it," she whispered, her voice low and trembling, filled with dread. She could see it now—beneath the surface of the Loom, the threads of fate began to twist and writhe, like serpents in the dark. The Loom was alive, but it was being *consumed*.

Aris's face tightened, and his hand moved to her shoulder, squeezing it with a strength that belied the terror she saw in his eyes. "We can't let it do this, Lyra. We have to reach the Loom first. If we don't—"

He didn't finish his sentence. There was no need to. They both knew what was at stake.

The Loom was their last hope. If they couldn't stop the Void from rethreading the world, from remaking it in its image—*in silence and ash*—then all would be lost. The threads of fate would be severed completely, and everything would fall into the nothingness that had been creeping up around them for so long.

Lyra's heart raced as they approached the Loom, but the closer they got, the more the air seemed to shift. The world around them grew colder, the earth beneath their feet harder, as though the very landscape was being stripped of its vitality. The Loom's dark presence seemed to suck the warmth from the air, leaving nothing but a hollow emptiness in its wake.

Her breath caught in her throat as she saw it—a twisting, roiling mass of darkness that was seeping into the Loom, into the threads that should have been pure, but now were knotted with shadows. It was the Void—*alive*—reaching into the heart of the Loom, rewriting the world with every breath it took.

"No," Lyra whispered, her voice barely a breath. "No, no, no…"

She felt the pull of the Void, as if it were calling her to join it, to surrender to the darkness and the silence it offered. The temptation was overwhelming—so much power, so much *control*. But she couldn't. She couldn't let it consume them both.

Her heart pounded as she reached out toward the Loom, the edges of her vision blurring with the intensity of the magic swirling around them. She could feel the song inside her, vibrating through her bones, her soul, but it was no longer the sweet, harmonious melody of fate. It had changed. The song was now a dissonant, painful thing, a screeching wail that echoed through her like a broken instrument. The Void was *inside* her now. It had been since the moment they'd stepped into the Rift, since the moment she had released the song to bind the threads.

"Aris," she gasped, her voice shaking. "It's… it's here. It's *too late*."

But Aris didn't stop. He kept walking, his steps steady, though she could see the strain in his jaw, the way his muscles tensed with the weight of their shared burden. "We haven't lost yet, Lyra. Not if we can reach it."

With every step, the air grew colder, heavier, and Lyra's fingers twitched at her sides. She could feel it—the Void was pulling at her, feeding off her uncertainty, her fear. It wanted to consume her. And in doing so, it would consume everything. It wanted to twist the song into its own dark image, to tear apart the threads of fate, to rewrite the world in its own distorted, silent vision.

"We can't let it win, Lyra," Aris said, his voice strained but full of determination. He reached for her hand, his fingers trembling as they closed around hers. "Together. We fight. Together."

She didn't have the words to answer him. She didn't need to. The Loom was ahead of them now, looming larger with each step, the darkness clinging to its massive frame, its gears frozen and still. The threads of fate that had once woven through it were now tangled, poisoned by the Void. Lyra's breath caught in her throat as she saw the way the Loom trembled, as if it were trying to fight back against the force that was seeping through its heart.

"We have to break the cycle," Lyra whispered, her voice tight, but full of resolve. "We have to *unweave* it."

Aris nodded. "Then let's do it."

They moved as one, their steps in sync as they approached the Loom. The air crackled with energy, the weight of their decision pressing down on them. The Void's song was loud now, a low, rumbling hum that filled the space around them, the sound of the world beginning to tear apart.

As they reached the base of the Loom, Lyra felt the magic inside her stir again, surging with purpose, but the temptation to surrender to the Void's darkness was still there, crawling at the edges of her mind. It was a call to let go, to stop fighting. The magic that swirled around her felt like it was trying to suffocate her, to drag her down into the abyss of nothingness.

But she couldn't.

Not after everything. Not after the choices they had made, the sacrifices they had borne together.

With a deep breath, Lyra extended her hands toward the Loom, her fingers brushing against the cold metal. She could feel the pulse of the threads inside it, distorted now by the Void's influence, but still *there*. The Loom was still alive, still capable of weaving, still capable of undoing the damage the Void had caused. But it needed *her*.

As her hands touched the Loom, the song inside her flared. The threads vibrated, singing once more—but this time, the song was not just hers. It was theirs, the power of their bond, their choices, weaving through the Loom like a thread of light in a sea of darkness.

The Void screamed.

The air turned ice-cold, and the ground beneath them cracked, the sound of breaking reality reverberating through the space. But Lyra and Aris held firm, their hands still gripping the Loom, the power between them surging as they fought against the darkness.

For a moment, it felt like they had won. Like the Loom would turn back the tide, rewrite fate and restore the world to what it had been. But the Void wasn't done. It never would be. It fought, clawing at the edges of the song, trying to consume it, to twist it into something else, something *dead*.

Lyra gasped, her breath ragged, as the strain of holding the threads in place began to take its toll. She could feel the power pulling her apart, the weight of the Void threatening to collapse her into itself. She reached for Aris's hand, their fingers entwined, and in that moment, she knew—*they would fight together*.

The Loom shuddered again, and the threads of fate began to hum once more, this time in harmony. They were winning. The song was growing stronger.

And as the Void howled in fury, Lyra whispered the final note.

The song was hers to shape. And with Aris by her side, the world was still theirs to *write*.

The world around them quaked as Lyra and Aris stood together, hands clasped, their wills aligned with the ancient Loom. The dark hum of the Void still filled the air, twisting the atmosphere with a sense of impending doom, but Lyra could feel the thread of her power growing stronger. The Loom was no longer just a machine. It was a living, breathing thing, a conduit for her will. She could feel the pulse of fate beating through it, like a heart, a rhythm that she could control.

Aris's grip tightened on her hand, and she turned to look at him. His face was pale, his brow drenched in sweat, but his eyes were unwavering. There was a quiet strength in him now, a fierce determination that matched her own. They had come so far, and the end was within their reach. But the Void—the darkness that had been lurking in the corners of their world—was not done with them yet.

The Loom trembled again, this time with more force. The threads beneath her fingers began to writhe, as if something was trying to break free from the fabric of reality itself. Lyra felt it—an irresistible pull, like gravity, dragging her down, threatening to tear her away from the Loom and from Aris. It was the Void, clawing at her, trying to reclaim what it had lost.

"No!" she gasped, clenching her teeth against the force of it. She pushed harder, focusing on the song that still resonated deep within her, pulling the power of the threads into her body, channeling it through her fingertips. The song was hers to wield, but she knew—she knew—if she didn't hold firm, if she didn't keep her focus, the Void would overwhelm them both.

"Lyra…" Aris whispered, his voice strained with effort, "we can't hold it forever. We need to finish this—now."

Her eyes met his, the bond between them crackling with the intensity of everything they had shared—the pain, the love, the broken trust, and the unspoken promises that lingered between them. They were at the edge of it all, standing together on the precipice of the world's rebirth. And yet, the truth was undeniable: *nothing* was certain. The Void still clung to the edges of reality, trying to rewrite the world in its image. But

Lyra refused to let that happen.

"We *will* finish it, Aris," she said, her voice steady despite the pounding in her chest. She took a deep breath, focusing on the song once more. The power was within her, within them. They had the strength to heal the Weave, to reset the broken threads of fate. "Together."

The Loom groaned beneath their hands, its metal structure pulsing with life as the threads began to twist and interlock, spinning around them like a living web. The world itself seemed to bend with it, as if the fabric of reality was being rewritten with every pulse of magic.

But then, the Void reached out once more. This time, it was different. It didn't just reach for the Loom. It reached for them. The air around them crackled, thick with the energy of the Void, and the very ground beneath their feet began to splinter, as though the world was being torn apart from the inside.

Lyra gasped, her fingers trembling against the Loom's surface. She could feel the darkness seeping into her, into the song, and for a moment, it felt as though it might swallow them whole. The threads beneath her hands began to unravel, pulling apart at the seams, and Lyra's heart pounded in her chest.

"Aris," she whispered, her voice barely audible. "It's trying to tear us apart."

He stepped closer, his body a shield against the force of the Void. His hands clasped hers tighter, and he pressed his forehead against hers. "Lyra, listen to me," he said, his voice firm. "We can't let it win. We have to *choose* to rewrite this. You don't have to fight it alone. I'm with you."

She closed her eyes, letting his words wash over her. She could feel the weight of everything pressing down on them—

the world, the Loom, the threads of fate—and yet, she knew. She knew that this was the moment where they would either save the world or watch it crumble to dust. She had the power, yes. But it wasn't just her power. It was *their* power. The bond between them, the strength they drew from each other, was the key.

The song inside her flared again, a brilliant, burning pulse that reverberated through the Loom and into the very fabric of the world itself. The Void recoiled, its tendrils snapping back as the song pushed against it, fighting to reclaim what had been lost.

"This is our choice, Lyra," Aris said, his voice now steady and unwavering. "We can make the world whole again, but it will require all of us. Not just the Loom. Not just the song. *Us.* Together."

Her breath caught in her throat, and she opened her eyes to meet his. There was no fear in his gaze now. There was only trust. Trust in her. Trust in them.

The Void howled again, louder this time, but Lyra didn't flinch. She could feel the threads of fate, the magic of the Loom, surging through her, feeding off the power of their shared bond. Together, they were stronger than the darkness.

Her hands pressed harder against the Loom, and the power surged once more. The song, the threads, the Loom—it all came together in a single, resounding pulse. The Void screamed in defiance, but it was too late. The magic of the Loom began to unwind the darkness, turning the Void's song back on itself.

The light flared around them, a burst of brilliance that illuminated the entire clearing. The Void writhed, its tendrils snapping and dissolving as the song of fate overtook it, rewriting the world with each passing second. The Loom spun, its gears turning with newfound purpose, and the very air shimmered with the power of creation.

For a moment, everything was silent. The world stood still, suspended in that breath between notes, as if the entire universe was waiting for something—waiting for the song to finish.

Then, slowly, the world began to breathe again. The threads of fate, once broken and tangled, were now woven back together. The Loom had undone the damage. The Weave had been restored.

Lyra felt the magic settle inside her, the song no longer a force of destruction, but a force of balance, of healing. She could feel the world shifting beneath her, like a deep breath being drawn after a long, aching silence.

But in the quiet aftermath, something else tugged at her heart.

The price. The cost. The sacrifice.

The Void had been defeated. The Loom had been reset. But Lyra could feel the subtle shift, the weight of something that had been taken. Something precious. Something that had been a part of her.

Her memory of the past—of *them*—was gone.

She turned to Aris, her eyes searching his, but something was different now. There was a faint distance between them, a gap where their shared history had once lived. The bond was still there, yes. But the memories? The moments they had shared? They felt *distant*. Like echoes from a life she could no longer reach.

Aris reached out to her, his hand brushing hers, but there was a quiet sadness in his eyes. "Lyra…" His voice was gentle, his expression aching. "We did it. Together. We saved it."

She nodded, but the words wouldn't come. She could feel the weight of their shared past pressing down on her, but it felt… *hollow*. The memories were no longer hers to hold. The world had been saved, but something precious had been lost in the process.

"Aris…" she whispered, her voice breaking with the realization. "I remember *us*, but I don't remember everything. Not the way I should."

He nodded, his expression softening with understanding. "It's all right, Lyra. We've rewritten fate. We've built something new. And no matter what happens, no matter what memories we've lost, we will always have each other."

Lyra took a deep breath, trying to steady herself. The Loom was quiet now, the threads of fate humming softly in the background. The world had been restored, but the price of memory still weighed heavily on her heart.

Together, they had saved the world. Together, they had rewritten fate.

But what would they become now?

What would their future look like, if the past could no longer be remembered?

Lyra and Aris stood in the quiet aftermath, their hands still intertwined, their hearts still bound by the song they had woven together. And though the memories were gone, the love they had shared—was still alive.

Seventeen

Love is a Dissonant Thread

The wind howled through the hollowed-out remnants of the world, carrying with it the scent of ash and the distant cries of things lost. The sky above them was a swirl of grey and red, torn between the battle of light and darkness that seemed to stretch across eternity. Lyra felt the weight of the Void pressing down on them both, the suffocating silence that had come to represent the destruction of everything she had known, and everything she had loved.

Beside her, Aris moved with slow, deliberate steps, his face pale, his body marked with the faint traces of the battle they had fought. He was still strong, still standing—but she could see it. The exhaustion in his eyes, the way he staggered slightly with each step. The wound on his side, where the darkness had lashed out at him, was still raw, bleeding, its black tendrils twisting into his skin.

"You're hurt," Lyra whispered, her voice barely audible above the roar of the Void.

"I'm fine," Aris replied through clenched teeth, his breath shallow. He tried to push himself upright, but his legs wavered, and for a moment, she thought he might fall. "It's nothing. We've come too far. We can't stop now."

The Void had reached its final form, a swirling vortex of silence and destruction, a wound in the very fabric of fate. It tore at the edges of the Weave, unraveling everything in its wake, devouring memories, lives, time. Its presence was overwhelming, the song of creation lost beneath its suffocating silence. Lyra felt the weight of its power pressing on her chest, the deep ache in her heart as it continued to distort everything around them.

But she couldn't stop. They couldn't stop.

The Loom had failed them. The threads of fate were tangled, and the world they had fought so hard to restore was on the brink of annihilation. The Void was not just an absence—it was alive now, a sentient force that devoured everything in its path. Its hunger had no end.

"I won't let you die, Aris," Lyra said, her voice fierce with determination.

He glanced at her then, his eyes dark with pain and something deeper—something that went beyond fear. It was the quiet, inevitable acceptance of what they had always known: nothing was ever truly safe, not for them, not for the world. But it was that same deep bond that had pulled them through the hardest of moments—the same unspoken love that had held them when words failed.

"We're in this together," he whispered, his lips curling into a faint, but desperate smile. "No matter what happens… we fight. Together."

Lyra nodded, swallowing the knot of emotion in her throat. The song, that once comforting melody, was now a broken thing, a dissonant hum in the back of her mind. She could feel it, the fragments of it still alive inside her, ready to burst free. But it wasn't enough. It wasn't strong enough to fight the Void.

She could hear it now—the Void's song. It was not a true song. It was an absence, a hollow void of all things, its notes out of tune, broken, as though it was trying to mimic the song of creation but failing at every turn. The Void was trying to take everything—*everything*—and make it nothing.

"Aris," she said, her voice steady despite the storm raging in her heart. "We need to break it. We need to *sing*."

He shook his head, his breath ragged as he swayed. "It's too late. The Void won't stop. It'll consume everything, Lyra. It's beyond repair."

"No." Her voice cracked, but she steadied herself. "It's never beyond repair."

She reached for him then, her hands shaking as she touched his chest, where the blood stained his tunic, soaking through. The wound was deep. His breathing was shallow, but he met her gaze, his dark eyes flickering with something that felt like a goodbye.

"I'll be fine," he whispered, though the words held no conviction. He couldn't even sit up now, his strength fading. "I'll be fine if you… just finish this. You have to. *For us.* For everyone."

Lyra closed her eyes, her fingers pressing against his skin, trying to hold him steady. There was no time for tears, no time for regret. She had made her choice—again. It was always the same choice. Aris was everything to her, the thread that had bound her to this world. She wouldn't let him fade, not without fighting. Not without giving everything she had.

And so she sang.

Not with words. Not with the melody she had once known. But with memory. Pain. Love.

The sound that left her lips was not a song of creation, but of everything they had lost. It was a cry of desperate longing, of everything they had fought for, everything they had been— together. Her voice shattered the silence, broken but filled with the power of the past, and as it spilled from her, it carried everything with it: the fear, the grief, the love, the sacrifice.

It was a song of the *end*, and the *beginning*.

As the first note left her lips, the world around them trembled. The Void flinched, its twisting mass recoiling slightly, but it did not stop. It *pushed* forward, relentlessly, its roar rising in a maddening cacophony.

"Lyra!" Aris shouted, his voice strained, weak. He was trying to sit up, but the blood loss, the exhaustion—it was too much. He reached out for her, but his hand fell limply to the side. His gaze flickered, his breath shallow, and in that moment, Lyra could feel the crack in his chest, the brokenness. He was fading.

And still, the song surged through her. She could feel it, the weight of the world, the weight of all they had lost, pulsing in her veins, trying to hold together the unraveling threads. It was not enough. She *was* the song of fate, but even her love, even her pain, was not enough to stop the darkness.

"No…" she whispered, desperation creeping into her voice. "Not enough. Not enough."

But then, something inside her shifted. A thread, a connection—between her and Aris—flickered, weak, but alive. She reached for it. She *pulled* it. And in that moment, a chord of memory, of love, struck within her chest.

The song—the real song—was not just power. It was not just magic. It was the *shared* breath between them. The melody of the soul, of who they were together.

The song wasn't meant to destroy. It was meant to *build*.

She grasped onto that truth, and the next note that escaped her lips was different. The Void shuddered, a deep crack opening across the dark expanse, its song faltering.

But it was not enough.

Her breath hitched as she felt Aris's grip slacken, his fingers slipping from hers. His chest barely rose with each breath. His voice—a whisper of a plea—escaped him. "Finish it, Lyra… please… finish it."

She couldn't speak. Her song choked in her throat, every breath a gasp of pain as she pulled the threads of fate tighter around her, around them. She closed her eyes, letting the memories flood her—of every moment with him. Every choice. Every sacrifice.

And in that fragile moment between breaths, as the song wove between them, Lyra felt her heart break.

She *sang*—not for herself, not even for Aris—but for everything they could have been. For the world they had tried to save.

The song cracked the Void. She felt it tear apart in her chest, felt the threads loosen, unraveling in the light of her love.

But it wasn't enough.

It was only a crack. And the Void still pushed forward.

Lyra's breath was a wheeze, her body trembling, but the song was still alive. It wasn't finished. It couldn't be. There had to be more.

And yet, as Aris's limp hand fell from hers, and the light in his eyes began to fade, the only thing Lyra could do was continue. The only choice left was to sing.

And somewhere, deep in the crack that she had created in the Void, she swore she heard a note in return.

The song, *their song*, had made its mark.

The Void recoiled, its twisting mass faltering as Lyra's song cracked against it, but it wasn't enough. Her breath caught in her chest, the pain surging through her as she watched Aris, so close yet slipping further away. His life, like the threads of fate, was fraying with each second. His body, once so full of strength and warmth, was growing cold, his pulse weaker with every passing moment.

The song, *their song*, echoed through her, but it was no longer the gentle melody of creation. It had become something else entirely—something jagged, something raw and fractured. The dissonance of it tore at her heart, the power of the song still surging, but she could feel it weakening.

Aris's eyes were half-closed now, his breath shallow. His fingers twitched, reaching for her, but the light in his gaze was dimming. He was still there—still *fighting*—but he was losing. She could feel it. He was slipping away.

"Aris, please… don't leave me," Lyra whispered, her voice raw, breaking under the weight of what she was about to lose.

She took his hand in hers once more, squeezing it desperately, as if she could pull him back from the edge. But his grip was weak, his strength fading with each beat of her heart. The Void was still fighting, still trying to swallow them whole. She could feel its cold tendrils wrapping around her, trying to pull her into the abyss.

Not yet, she thought fiercely. *I won't let you go.*

Her voice trembled as she sang again—not with power, but with *everything*. She poured her heart into the song, the love they had shared, the loss she felt as Aris faded, as the world they had tried to save crumbled to dust. The song surged from her chest, a cry that was more than magic—it was pure, unfiltered emotion. It was the breath of a broken heart.

Her song filled the air, the sound of it bending reality, twisting the fabric of fate itself. The Void screamed, a deep, guttural howl that shook the earth beneath their feet, but it wasn't enough. The cracks Lyra had created, the fractures in the Void, were healing—closing. The darkness was reclaiming the world.

Lyra couldn't stop it. She couldn't let him go.

"I'm sorry, Aris," she whispered through her tears. "I'm sorry I can't save you. But I will not stop. I will not—"

A low groan rumbled beneath their feet. The Void was fighting back, but this time, Lyra could feel something— *something different*. The Void's song was faltering, its power wavering, and for the first time, she felt a flicker of hope.

I'm still here, she thought, *I'm still fighting.*

Her hand trembled as it clutched Aris's, but it wasn't just the Void she was fighting anymore. It was the pull of her own heart, the realization that no matter what she did, no matter how hard she fought, the world would change. Aris would change. And they would never go back to what they had been.

Her song twisted and turned, discordant but powerful, raw and beautiful in its chaos. It was a battle of wills now. The song of creation, of fate, of *love*—against the Void, against the darkness that sought to rewrite it all.

But Lyra felt a tug at her soul, a spark of light at the center of the chaos.

And with that spark, something inside her began to *shift*.

The Void trembled once more, its dark tendrils snapping back, but this time, it wasn't just an absence. It was *retreating*. Lyra's eyes widened, a fragile flicker of light breaking through the blackness. The threads of fate—tangled, broken, and twisted—began to weave themselves back together. Not perfectly, not yet, but it was enough. The threads had life again.

Eighteen

The Final Looming

The Loom stood before them, a monument to the last hope of the world, its great gears whirring faintly as if sensing the gravity of the choice ahead. It towered like a relic from an age long forgotten, an ancient machine that had once been the heart of the Weavers, the source of fate's threads. Now, it was broken, twisted by the Void's touch. But within it lay the possibility of restoration—the key to healing the world that had been torn asunder.

Lyra felt the pull, deep in her chest, a breathless weight that dragged her forward, step by agonizing step. Her fingers trembled at her sides, and despite the urgency in her heart, the air around her was thick with the gravity of the choice that loomed ahead. The Loom was not just a machine. It was alive, humming with the remnants of magic, of power that could rewrite the world. But to restore it, to finalize the weave of fate, one of them had to give up everything—*forever*.

She stole a glance at Aris beside her, his face set in an expression she knew all too well. The hardness in his jaw, the way his eyes never left the Loom, were signs of a man who had already made up his mind. She could see the resolution in him, the burden he carried as he prepared himself for the sacrifice. His bloodied hands, the signs of the battles they had fought, were no longer his concern. There was only the Loom now. Only the end of this fight.

But Lyra would not let him. Not again. Not after everything they had shared, after everything they had fought for.

"You don't have to do this," she whispered, though her voice cracked with the weight of her own uncertainty. The wind around them howled, a reminder of the chaos they had fought to hold at bay. The Void still threatened the edges of the world, and the Loom was their only chance. But this—*this*—felt like the breaking point, the line that separated everything they were from everything they would ever be.

Aris looked at her, his expression softening just for a moment. "It's the only way, Lyra. The only way to fix it. The Loom demands a sacrifice—*one* of us, to complete the weave. It's me. I'm the one who should do it."

His words hit her like a physical blow. The Loom's hum seemed to grow louder as though it were calling to him, to *them*, pulling them into its grasp, demanding the completion of the song. But Lyra couldn't bear it—not again. Not after everything they had already given up.

"No," she said, her voice gaining strength. "No, Aris. I won't let you. I won't let you sacrifice yourself for me again."

His eyes softened, but the resolve remained in them. "You don't have a choice, Lyra. The Loom demands one of us. If I don't do it, we lose everything."

She shook her head, the tears she had held back for so long now threatening to spill. "You're wrong. We don't have to lose anything. *We* can finish this together. We've always fought together. Always."

Aris's gaze softened, and for a brief moment, Lyra saw the pain in him, the love that still burned between them despite everything that had happened. He stepped closer to her, his hand reaching out to grasp hers. She could feel the heat of his touch, the pulse of life still strong in him, despite the way the world was crumbling around them.

"You don't understand," he murmured, his voice tight with something she couldn't quite place. "If I do this—if I become part of the Loom—then the world will be whole again. I can't let you bear that burden, Lyra. It's not your choice to make."

Her heart broke. She couldn't breathe. She didn't want to lose him. Not like this. Not after everything. She had already lost him once—had watched him fade away into the darkness of the Void. The thought of him sacrificing himself for this cause, for *her*, tore her apart.

"No, Aris," she whispered, stepping forward, closing the distance between them. "I *won't* lose you again. We've come this far together. We fight together. And this, too, we will do together."

The Loom hummed louder now, its power growing with every word they spoke, every moment that passed. Lyra could feel the pressure in the air, the tension crackling between them, as the Loom's magic began to pull at the very fabric of their being. She could feel the final piece of fate slipping into place, the one moment that would define the rest of their lives.

"I will do it," Aris insisted, his voice low, but filled with finality. "This is my choice. I made it."

"You don't get to make this choice alone." Her voice was a whisper, but it felt like a command. "*I* choose, too."

The song—their song—was still alive within her, a melody of creation and destruction, of love and loss. The dissonant chords that had defined their bond were still there, raw and jagged, but now, as she stood in the shadow of the Loom, she could feel something shifting inside her. She wasn't just *Lyra*—the Weaver of Endings. She was *Lyra*, bound to Aris. And she refused to let him slip away. Not again.

The wind howled once more, but this time it wasn't just the wind. It was the song—cracking, breaking free from the chains they had held it in. The Void was still there, its tendrils scraping at the edges of the world, but it was weakening. The Loom had the power to stop it, to complete the weave, but it would cost them both.

"I won't let you sacrifice yourself," she said, her voice shaking with emotion. "Not again. Not after everything. We finish this together. *Together*, Aris."

And in that moment, Lyra realized something. The Loom, the world, the threads of fate—they were not meant to be woven by one alone. They were meant to be *shared*. Two souls, bound by love, by choice, by memory. It was their song. Together, they had built it, fought for it, and now— together—they would complete it.

Aris opened his mouth to protest, but she silenced him with a finger pressed gently to his lips. Her touch lingered for a moment, and the world around them seemed to pause, the air heavy with their shared breath. And then, she did the only thing she could do.

She began to sing.

Not with words. Not with power alone. But with the

memory of them. With the love they shared, the pain they had endured, and the choice they had made. The song rose from her, breaking through the tension in the air, the dissonance of their love, and it was a song of *togetherness.*

Aris's hand slipped into hers, his fingers trembling, but he didn't pull away. He joined her. His voice—faint, raw, but filled with everything he had—blended with hers, and together, they sang the melody of fate. It was a duet—a harmony forged from pain, from sacrifice, from love.

The Loom began to vibrate in time with their song. The threads of fate, once broken, began to weave themselves back together, the dark tendrils of the Void receding with every note they sang. The world around them shimmered, as if the fabric of existence was folding and unfolding in response to their power.

But it wasn't enough. The Void, though weaker, was still fighting, still clawing at the world they were trying to save.

Lyra's breath came faster now, the strain of the magic pulsing through her, threatening to consume her. She could feel Aris's pulse, his strength fading, and she knew. She *knew* the price they had to pay. But she refused to let it be his life again. *Not again.*

She sang louder, pouring everything into the song, calling not just for herself, not just for Aris, but for the world—for the memory of all they had fought for. Her voice cracked with the intensity of it, but she pushed through. She could feel Aris's breath steady beside hers, and together they fought the darkness with everything they had.

The Loom *shuddered* under the weight of their song, the threads of fate knitting themselves together in intricate patterns, healing the rift, but it wasn't enough. The final thread—

the one that would bind them to the Loom, forever—was still missing.

Lyra knew the truth. She couldn't avoid it anymore. The Loom demanded a final sacrifice.

And it wasn't just Aris's sacrifice to make.

She sang the final note, calling both their names—*together*.

The Void howled one last time, but it could not hold. The Loom, powered by their song, finally completed the weave, the threads of fate now whole again.

But as the last note faded, Lyra felt a sharp, aching emptiness. The sacrifice had been made.

And though the world had been saved, there was still one thing left hanging in the balance.

What would they become now?

The final note hung in the air like a breath, suspended between the echoes of the past and the fragile threads of the future. Lyra's chest heaved with the weight of the song, her body trembling from the intensity of the magic, but as the last note faded, something shifted inside her. The Loom, now alive with the energy of their shared song, began to hum louder, its gears grinding against the stillness, turning slowly, pulling fate back into its rightful place. Yet in the wake of the magic, a stillness fell over them.

The world around them had changed. The Void was retreating, its tendrils unraveling in the wind, fading away like smoke dissipating in the dawn. But even as the air around them grew calmer, even as the Loom's hum turned to a soothing rhythm, there was a stillness between Lyra and Aris that stretched like an invisible wall between them.

Lyra pulled her hand away from his, unwilling to let it go but unable to keep it there. The magic had done its work, and she could feel it in the way the world around them was shifting. The rift was healing, the threads of fate knitting themselves back together, but the price had been paid.

Her heart clenched in her chest.

It was him. It was always him.

Aris stood motionless, his face blank but his eyes reflecting the flickering light of the Loom, his breath labored and shallow. He had given everything to make this possible. She knew that. She *knew* that.

But the song they had just sung was more than just magic. It was an emotional tapestry woven from pain, sacrifice, and the love they had shared. That love had always been their strength, and in that moment, Lyra could feel it unraveling—bit by bit. There had been a sacrifice, a price neither of them could avoid.

As the last remnants of the Void faded away, Lyra felt the absence of the bond between them. It was subtle at first, but it grew. The threads that had once woven their fates together were no longer as taut. The intensity of their connection—so fierce, so consuming—was now softening, like the last embers of a fire that was slowly dying out.

And then, she realized.

Aris was *no longer* beside her in the same way. He was there physically, yes, standing before her, his hand still stretched out, but something was different. The energy between them had shifted. She could feel it like a cold wind sweeping through her chest.

"Aris…" she whispered, her voice wavering with uncertainty, her eyes searching his face.

He didn't answer immediately. His lips parted, but no words came. He seemed lost in the new silence that had settled around them, the hum of the Loom still resonating, but the world—*their world*—felt quieter than it had ever been before.

A crack formed in her chest, deep and aching, as her heart fought against the truth that was slowly revealing itself. The Loom had given them their chance to rebuild the world, but it had taken something else.

"Aris, what's happening?" she asked, her voice soft but desperate. Her fingers hovered over his hand, but she couldn't quite bring herself to touch him.

His eyes met hers, and for a fleeting moment, Lyra saw something—something raw and vulnerable—before it was masked by an unreadable expression. "I think..." he began, his voice hoarse, "I think the sacrifice was more than I expected. The Loom, it..." He trailed off, his gaze flickering down to the ground, his hands shaking at his sides.

"No..." Lyra breathed, a sharp pain flooding her chest as she realized. She stepped back, her eyes widening with the dawning realization. "No, Aris. You—*you* are the sacrifice. You gave yourself to the Loom."

He nodded, slowly, his face pale. "I didn't think it would cost so much. I thought we could fix it together, Lyra. I thought..."

His words faltered, and for a moment, he couldn't continue. Lyra's heart raced as she reached out to him, but the space between them felt vast, as though an unseen force was pushing her away. She didn't know how to fix this, how to mend the bond that had suddenly snapped. The Loom had given them hope, but it had also taken him from her in ways she hadn't expected.

"You—" she began, but the words stuck in her throat. Her mind was reeling. She felt the song still inside her, still pulsing, but it wasn't the same. The dissonance was sharper now, and she could feel the pain of the world pressing down on her like the weight of a collapsing star.

Aris reached for her, but as his fingers brushed against hers, there was no spark. No pull. It was a faint connection, nothing like it had been before. A mere whisper of what had once been an unbreakable bond.

"Lyra, I'm sorry," Aris said, his voice heavy with sorrow. "I thought I could save you—save us. But the Loom… it took more than I thought. I thought I could protect you from this."

Her chest tightened, the pressure building to an unbearable intensity. The song was *broken* now, shattered by the very thing that had once held them together. The Loom had taken his essence, bound him to it forever. The price of restoring fate was not just his life, but his existence as he had known it. He was here, but *not*. He was with her, but *distant*. The magic had rewritten the very fabric of their bond, and now—now the threads between them were weakening.

"You've *already* sacrificed yourself," Lyra said, her voice shaking. "Don't you understand? The Loom took you, Aris. It bound you to its heart. And now—now I'm losing you again."

He closed his eyes, and the agony of it flashed across his face. "You'll never lose me, Lyra. I'm still here. I'm still with you." His hand fell away from hers, and it felt like the last thread had snapped. He didn't reach for her again.

"Then why does it feel like you're already gone?" Her voice cracked as the floodgates opened, her tears blurring her vision.

Aris didn't answer. He didn't need to.

The Loom was healing, the world was being restored, but the price had been paid, and Lyra was left with nothing but the echo of what had been. The love they had shared, the bond that had once been unbreakable, had been torn apart. Aris had given his essence to the Loom—he had woven himself into the fabric of fate, and now he was part of the threads that held the world together. He was still *there*, but not *with her*. Not the way he had been.

She felt it then—the final, sharp tear of the thread between them. The magic that had once brought them together now kept them apart, and Lyra, no longer able to stand the weight of it, staggered back, gasping for breath as she felt the world slip away.

"Lyra…" Aris whispered her name, his voice thin, distant.

She couldn't answer him. She couldn't move. There was no song left in her. Only silence.

The Loom hummed steadily behind them, the weight of fate reshaping the world, but in that moment, Lyra knew that no matter what they had fought for—no matter how hard they had tried—some things could never be rewritten.

Love, it seemed, was a dissonant thread, twisted and torn beyond repair.

And they were left to wonder if anything could ever be whole again.

Nineteen

When Fates Drown in Silence

The Loom shuddered violently, the sound like a thousand strings being plucked all at once—sharp, discordant, a breaking point where all things converged and shattered. The earth beneath them trembled as if the world itself were trying to tear free from the threads that bound it. Lyra's heart raced, her breath shallow, as the Loom's massive gears groaned in protest. The air crackled with raw, wild magic, the weight of destiny itself collapsing into a singular moment.

Everything was falling apart.

She clutched Aris's hand tightly, her fingers intertwined with his, as they stood before the Loom—no longer the monument to fate, but a ticking, splintering machine that was coming undone. She could feel the song still within her, but it was fading, silenced by the crash of destruction that enveloped them. The threads—the delicate threads that had woven fate into existence—were unraveling, snapping like brittle ropes under a heavy load. The Void, the endless darkness that had threatened to consume them all, was pulling at the very fabric of reality. But the Loom—*the Loom*—had never been more alive, thrumming with a chaotic energy that demanded release.

"No, no, no…" Lyra gasped, her voice barely a whisper above the sound of the world breaking. She could feel it—the thread of fate, the binding magic, slipping away from her. Aris's grip on her hand tightened, but she could feel him fading too. The darkness was pulling at them both, and there was no way to stop it now. The Loom was coming undone.

Aris's face, once so full of determination and hope, was now twisted with pain. His eyes were wide, his mouth parted in a silent cry as the explosion of energy from the Loom reached its peak. The song they had both been bound to—their shared creation—was no longer enough. It was slipping from them.

"I won't let you go, Lyra," Aris whispered hoarsely, but his voice seemed distant, as though it came from another world, one she could no longer reach. He was still there, still with her, but his presence was fading. He was slipping through the cracks, like sand falling between fingers.

"Don't leave me," Lyra begged, her voice breaking. "Please, Aris. I *can't*—"

But it was too late.

The Loom exploded with a force so great that Lyra was thrown backward, her body crashing to the ground. The world seemed to collapse into a single instant of blinding light, and then—the silence.

It was immediate. Absolute. All-consuming.

The air that had once been filled with the buzz of magic, the hum of fate weaving itself together, was now silent. So silent that it pressed against her eardrums, like the void between two breaths. The explosion of energy had burned away the very fabric of reality, leaving only stillness in its wake.

Lyra sat up slowly, disoriented. Her chest rose and fell with shallow breaths, her body shaking from the aftershock. Her eyes blurred with the remnants of the explosion, the echo of light and sound still pulsing in her mind. She couldn't hear anything. No hum, no song. Only silence.

And then, slowly, a new sound began to fill the air. A soft, distant melody—pure and sweet, as though the world itself had decided to sing again. A lullaby of life, of creation, of the song that had been lost and now, in the quiet aftermath of destruction, was returning.

Lyra blinked, her vision clearing. She could see the sky above her—a brilliant blue, untouched by the chaos. The earth beneath her was solid, unchanged, and yet it felt different. The air was warmer, the light softer. Everything was in place, but it felt like she had stepped into a different world—a world that was whole again, healed, but eerily silent.

The first note of the song—a single, delicate sound—wrapped around her, filling her chest, and for the first time in what felt like an eternity, Lyra felt *peace*.

But then her gaze flickered to the space beside her, and the world around her stopped.

Aris was not there.

Her breath caught in her throat as her pulse raced in panic. She reached out, her hands trembling, her fingers brushing against the cool grass beneath her. The absence of his presence was an ache she couldn't explain. The air was still, the song still lingering, but Aris… Aris was gone.

She stood quickly, her eyes frantically searching the empty

landscape around her. The sky was perfect, the world pristine, but he was nowhere to be seen. The world had been restored, but without him. Without *them*.

"Aris!" Lyra shouted, her voice cracking as it echoed through the silent world. "Aris, where are you?"

But there was no answer.

The wind whispered, but it was a soft, mournful sound, as though the earth itself was mourning with her. The song—this beautiful, quiet melody—was all that remained, and yet it filled her with dread, for she knew what it meant. It meant Aris was *gone*. The threads of fate had been woven, the world had been healed, but at a price she couldn't comprehend. He had given everything to stop the Void. He had sacrificed himself, and she had failed to stop him. Now, the Loom was complete, but it had taken him with it.

Her hand reached up to her chest, to where she could feel the song vibrating within her. The connection to the Loom—the last piece of the magic—was still alive within her, but it felt hollow. She could feel the world shifting, the threads of fate realigning, but there was something missing. Something vital. Something *irreplaceable*.

A sound broke the silence then—faint at first, a soft rustling sound. Lyra's heart leapt as she turned toward it, but her hope quickly faded as she saw what it was: a single golden thread, fluttering in the wind like a delicate ribbon.

She knelt down, her fingers trembling as she reached for it. The thread was warm to the touch, its shimmer soft and radiant, as though it were made of starlight. It was beautiful, fragile, and for a brief moment, Lyra allowed herself to believe that it might be Aris—that this thread might be the last remnant of him, a piece of his essence.

But as her fingers closed around it, she realized with a crushing weight that it was more than that. It was *his* thread, yes—but it was the thread of fate, the thread of all they had woven together. It was the last part of their shared song, now bound to her. Aris had become part of the very fabric of fate itself.

And yet…

The space where he had stood—where they had stood together—was empty.

A single tear slipped down Lyra's cheek as she held the golden thread in her palm, feeling its warmth radiate against her skin. The song filled the world once more, the melody as clear as a crystal, but it was a song without him. A song without the one person who had once been her everything.

"Aris…" she whispered, her voice breaking, lost in the silence. "Why?"

The thread pulsed in her palm, but it was no longer the same. It was his essence, yes, but it wasn't *him.* He was gone. The Loom had been completed, but at the cost of the man she loved. She had seen it all—the sacrifice, the breaking of fate—but the truth had never been clearer: *He had become part of the song, part of the Loom itself.*

A soft, melodic hum filled the air, and Lyra's gaze lifted to the horizon, where the golden thread seemed to catch the light, its shimmer casting a soft glow across the landscape. The world had been healed, the threads of fate woven back into their rightful place, but Aris was gone. The Loom had claimed him.

Yet, as she stood there, the faintest trace of a smile tugged at the corner of her lips, even as her heart cracked. Aris had become part of the world they had saved. His sacrifice, his love, had not been in vain. And in the quiet song of this new world, she could still hear him—a distant echo, like the wind singing through the trees.

The song was not over.

The song was only beginning.

And though Aris was gone from her side, Lyra knew that the threads of fate would continue to weave. She would carry his memory within her, the golden thread pulsing softly in her palm, and she would live. For him. For them both.

The peace of the world was heavy, but it was hers now.

The silence, the peace—it was theirs.

Lyra stood alone in the stillness of the world, her breath ragged as she clutched the golden thread in her hand, feeling its pulse against her skin like the beat of a heart. The world around her shimmered, untouched, as if frozen in time, but it felt unfamiliar. The land was whole again, the scars of the Void retreating into the earth, but without Aris by her side, the emptiness was more profound than any destruction the Void could bring.

The thread shimmered in her palm, warm and fragile, a remnant of a life that had once been. She closed her fingers around it, the heat of it burning through her, searing into her skin. There was something about this thread, this piece of him, that felt alive—alive in a way that she couldn't fully grasp. It was as though the thread contained all that he had been: his strength, his sacrifice, his love for her.

But it wasn't him.

It wasn't *Aris*.

The weight of that truth crushed her chest.

She took a trembling step forward, but the world around her felt distant, muted. The song that had once filled the air, that had connected them both, was now nothing but a whisper on the wind. She reached out, but there was nothing to touch, nothing to grasp. The Loom had been destroyed, reshaped, but it was no longer part of her. Aris had given himself to it, sacrificed everything—*for them*—and now the Loom was no more.

A sudden chill raced down her spine, and the air around her shifted. The silence pressed in on her, squeezing the breath from her lungs. There was no hum of magic now, no force of fate pulling at the edges of reality. It was quiet. Too quiet.

And yet, despite the void that stretched between her and the rest of the world, Lyra could still hear the faintest echo of something. A whisper in the wind.

Lyra.

Her heart skipped a beat, and she spun around, her breath catching in her throat. The sound of her name had been faint, like a fleeting memory she couldn't quite hold onto, but it was there. A voice—*his* voice—so soft, yet so familiar.

"Aris?" she called, her voice trembling, but the world around her remained silent, the wind picking up around her, pushing her forward.

The golden thread in her hand pulsed again, more strongly now, the warmth deepening, as if it were reaching out to her. It was the only sign left of him. The only piece she had left to hold on to.

Without thinking, Lyra gripped the thread tighter and closed her eyes. She could still feel the power of their shared song, still hear the faint echo of their love resonating in the back of her mind. She had always known that fate was never simple, that the world they had lived in was fragile. But now, now it seemed as if she had crossed the threshold into something *other*, something neither fully light nor dark, and the only way out was to complete the song—*their* song.

A soft, low hum began to vibrate beneath her feet, a ripple running through the earth. The ground trembled once more, not with destruction, but with the pulse of the golden thread. The Loom had been undone, yes, but what remained, what they had *woven* together, was still alive. It was more than magic. It was the very fabric of existence.

A sudden weight pressed upon Lyra's chest, but it wasn't pain—it was *presence*. The thread of gold in her palm seemed to glow brighter now, filling the empty space around her with warmth, with light.

And then, in that breathless instant, Lyra felt something—someone—shift beside her.

Her eyes flew open.

Aris stood before her, or at least, his shape, his presence, was there—his figure blurred, shimmering in the light of the Loom's final breath, but *it was him*. His image flickered like a mirage, his silhouette outlined in gold and shadow. His face was indistinct, but his eyes—his eyes—were filled with the same warmth she had known, the same depth of emotion that had always been there between them.

"Aris…" she whispered, her voice breaking. She reached out, but the figure before her seemed to fade, like smoke caught in the wind. The air was thick with magic, but it wasn't solid. It was a memory, a vision—a fragment of him trapped in the threads she held.

His voice came to her, barely a whisper: *"I'm here, Lyra. Always."*

She gasped, the truth of it surging through her. He was *here*. Not fully, not in the way she had once known, but he was alive, *within* her, within the very thread she held. The song had brought him back, not in form, but in *essence*. He had become the Loom. He had become part of the thread that wove fate.

"Aris, I…" Lyra's voice cracked as tears threatened to spill. She reached for the fading image of him, desperate to hold on to the last piece of him, but the vision began to slip through her fingers.

"I am still with you," his voice echoed in her mind, like a song that would never fade. "You've completed the song, Lyra. You've finished the weave. Fate has been restored, and I… I'm part of that now. I am with you, always."

The world around her shimmered, the edges of reality bending and distorting, and she felt it—the presence of him, not as a form to touch, but as a connection that spanned through her heart, through the threads of fate. The golden thread pulsed one last time, then unraveled in her hand, its light fading into the air, leaving behind the faintest trace of warmth.

Lyra fell to her knees, overwhelmed by the power of it. The song, the Loom, the world they had fought to restore—it was all alive. The threads were whole again. The song of fate had been rewritten. And even though Aris was no longer physically beside her, he was with her in the deepest, most essential way.

"I will carry you with me," she whispered, clutching the space where his presence had been, the echo of his voice still ringing in her heart. "I will carry *us* with me."

The air around her began to settle, the weight of the magic now peaceful, the world slowly returning to a calm, gentle hum. The land, the skies, the very air itself felt lighter, as though the tension had been released and the world was breathing again. The Void, that darkness that had tried to tear everything apart, was gone. And in its place was the soft glow of the Loom's magic, restored.

Lyra stood slowly, wiping away the tears that had fallen, her chest still aching but filled with something else. *Hope.* The world was healed. Fate had been woven anew. And though Aris was gone, his sacrifice had made this possible.

She looked to the horizon, where the golden light of a new day rose, filling the world with promise.

And in that quiet, sacred moment, Lyra knew that she would carry the song with her for as long as she lived—*their song*, the song of fate, of love, and of all that was and could be. The Loom had been completed, but the music would play on, forever.

Twenty

The Song That Was Never Sung

The marketplace was alive with sound.

It was an unfamiliar city, a place Lyra had never been, yet it was somehow strangely familiar. The air was thick with the scent of fresh bread and incense, the chatter of merchants haggling over their wares, and the distant laughter of children playing in the streets. But above it all, there was one sound that stood out—a melody, soft and sweet, threading its way through the chaos of the market.

Lyra paused in her steps, her heart skipping as the first few notes of the tune reached her ears. Her fingers twitched at her sides as she followed the sound, a familiar ache settling in her chest. It was a melody she knew too well—the melody of the song that had woven the threads of fate, the song that had tied her heart to Aris's. The same song that had been lost in the dark silence of the Void.

She pushed her way through the crowd, her breath shallow as

she searched for the source of the music. The song was almost the same—nearly identical to the one she had sung with Aris all those years ago, the one that had bound their souls together, that had kept them alive through the chaos. But it was different too, a faint variation in the notes, a slight shift that made the melody feel like a shadow of what it had once been.

And then, she saw him.

A young bard, no more than twenty, sitting on the stone steps of a nearby vendor stall. His eyes were closed, his fingers gently strumming a lute as the melody flowed from him, sweet and clear. Lyra's heart thudded in her chest as she took in the sight of him, the way the sunlight caught in his hair, the way the breeze teased the loose strands that fell across his forehead.

But it wasn't his appearance that stopped her breath. It was his eyes.

They were the same. The same eyes she had once loved, the same eyes that had looked at her with so much promise, so much warmth, so much *hope*. They were Aris's eyes.

Her heart clenched painfully, and she felt a rush of heat rise to her cheeks as the memories flooded back. Aris. Her love. Her heart, her soul, the man she had fought to save and the man who had become part of the Loom itself. The man she had lost.

The song he played was his. It was *theirs*, but he was not Aris. It wasn't possible. He couldn't be. This young man, this stranger, couldn't hold the weight of everything they had been. And yet, here he was, playing the tune that had been their salvation.

Lyra's fingers ached to reach out, to touch the music, to feel the pull of the song that still vibrated in her bones. She stepped closer, drawn as if by an invisible thread. The sound of the lute, the melody she had once shared with Aris, filled her ears again. Each note seemed to crack her open, making her wonder if this was real or some cruel trick of fate.

The bard's fingers stilled on the strings, and as if sensing her presence, his eyes opened slowly, their depths shining with curiosity. And for a fleeting moment, the world seemed to stop.

He looked at her, and in his gaze, Lyra saw something she could not name. His eyes held no recognition, no memory of her. No knowledge of the life they had shared. There was no glint of recognition in his expression, no spark of the shared bond they had once known.

But still, it was there. The pull. The inexplicable connection that stretched between them, pulling her toward him like gravity.

The silence between them stretched, thick and heavy, until the bard's lips parted, and he spoke.

"Do you know the song?" he asked, his voice soft, almost shy. It was familiar, but different, like a ghost of a forgotten melody. "It's an old one. My mother used to sing it to me when I was a child."

Lyra's heart thudded painfully in her chest, and she felt the blood rush to her ears as the world around her swayed. His voice was a tremor in the air, a fleeting echo of a past she thought she had lost forever. He didn't know. He couldn't know. He was a stranger. And yet...

"I…" Lyra began, her voice catching in her throat. Her breath came faster now, her hands trembling as the memories surged forward, crashing over her. "I know it," she whispered, the words slipping out before she could stop them. "I know it by heart."

The bard's eyebrows furrowed slightly, and his gaze dropped to the strings of his lute, his fingers moving slowly, thoughtfully, as if considering something. His head tilted to the side, a spark of recognition flickering in his expression.

"The song… it's strange," he said, his voice hesitant now, almost as though he were piecing something together. "I don't know why I can't stop playing it. It's like… like I've always known it, like it's been part of me. But…" His voice trailed off, and his eyes flickered back to hers. "But I don't know why it matters."

Lyra's breath caught in her throat. This… this was impossible. How could this be happening? She could feel it, a deep tug in her chest, a pull that was impossible to ignore. It was as if the song—their song—was calling her home.

The bard's fingers stilled on the lute strings, and he looked at her, truly looking at her for the first time. There was something in his eyes now—something deep and ancient, as though he was seeing her in a way that no one else ever had. His lips parted again, and this time, his voice was filled with wonder.

"Do you—do you feel it?" he asked, his gaze fixed on hers. "It's like—like we're meant to play this together. Like the song is calling us to finish it."

Lyra's heart stopped. The words were a confession, a revelation, but also a question—a question that reached into the very core of her. She wanted to answer, wanted to say something, but the weight of the moment, of everything that was unraveling, held her silent. Her chest was tight, her head spinning as the world seemed to bend around the stranger, around the music that played between them.

"I…" Lyra took a breath, her fingers itching to reach out. The golden thread, the song that had bound her and Aris together, was stirring in her soul again. It was the same tune. The same melody. The same rhythm that had once been their salvation.

No. Her heart raced with the realization. This wasn't just fate. This wasn't just coincidence.

She was here for a reason. He was here for a reason.

With trembling hands, Lyra stepped forward, her voice a whisper as she began to hum the next note. The sound was tentative at first, but as the melody flowed through her, she felt the tension between them shatter, like a dam breaking open.

The young bard's eyes widened, and before he could stop himself, he joined her. His voice was soft, unsure at first, but it blended with hers, the two of them creating a harmony so perfect that it filled the space between them, surrounding them with the magic of the past and the promise of the future.

And for a moment, the world around them *paused.* The market, the people, the sounds of life—they all faded as the song wrapped around them, binding their fates together, just as it had done so long ago.

Lyra closed her eyes, letting the music wash over her. She had never forgotten it. She had never forgotten *him.* Aris. And now, somehow, in the form of this young bard, the song was alive again, pulling her into the melody that had once defined her.

The bard sang with her, his voice more confident now, the song carrying them both as if it had always been meant for them to finish it.

And in the deep resonance of the final note, Lyra's heart soared, and a single tear slipped down her cheek.

The song that was never sung—was finally, at last, complete.

As the last note faded into the air, Lyra's eyes met the bard's, and for the first time since she had lost him, she felt the threads of fate tighten once more—this time, not as a final goodbye, but as a beginning.

The last note of their shared song echoed in the air, lingering like a soft, dying whisper that reverberated through the heart of the world. The market, the bustling life around them, seemed to fade into the background, as if the melody itself had held the world still for that one fleeting moment. Lyra stood there, eyes wide, breath shallow, the young bard's voice still ringing in her ears.

They were standing in the same place, but everything had shifted. The connection between them, the song they had just woven together, pulsed like a heartbeat, alive and trembling with the energy of something ancient and irrevocable. The thread of fate had been woven once again—this time, not by the Loom, but by their hands, their voices, their hearts. The magic was no longer just an echo of the past; it was *present*. The music had carried them across the impossible gap between yesterday and today, between life and death, between what had been and what could be.

The young bard's gaze softened as their song came to a close. His fingers lingered on the lute, but now, the melody had faded into silence, leaving an aftertaste of something more profound than sound.

"What is this?" Lyra whispered, her voice trembling. She had to ask, though the answer was already stirring in her chest, in her very bones. She could feel it, the pull between them, the connection that ran deeper than any melody or magic. His eyes—*Aris's eyes*—still held that unfathomable depth, but there was something else now, something familiar, a feeling she couldn't name.

The bard blinked, as if coming out of a trance. "I—don't know. I've always played that song. I just—just felt like it was something I had to do. I've never been able to stop playing it."

Lyra's heart pounded in her chest, her mind racing. She could feel the weight of the moment pressing down on her—like the first gust of wind before a storm, like the final breath of an age. There was something she needed to understand. Something she had known, deep within her, but had been too afraid to acknowledge until now.

"I've heard this song before," she said quietly, but her voice was firm. "I know it. It's the song of fate, the song of the Loom, the song of…" Her throat tightened. She forced herself to speak the words. "Of *us*."

The bard's gaze flickered to the ground, and for a moment, it was as though the world had come to a complete halt. He didn't respond, but there was something in his eyes—a quiet understanding, a recognition. He had been playing a melody for his entire life, a melody that had *always* been part of him, yet he had never known its meaning. And in this moment, standing before Lyra, the pieces were starting to fall into place.

Lyra stepped forward, her breath shaky as she reached out, her fingers trembling. "You…" She couldn't finish the thought. It was too much. Too overwhelming. Could it be? Could this be him? Could he—*Aris*—be here, in this new life, in this young man who carried his eyes, his song, but none of the memories that had once bound them together?

The bard's lips parted, but before he could speak, something shifted. Lyra's heart thudded in her chest as the song—*their song*—pulsed within her again. The connection, the bond that had tied her and Aris together for lifetimes, was stirring inside her like a flame rekindled from a dying ember.

"I..." The bard hesitated, his gaze searching hers as if he could feel the magic swirling between them. "I think... I think I know you."

The world around them shifted. The people of the market, the vendors, the children—everything resumed, the sounds of life filling the air again. But Lyra didn't hear them. All she could hear was the song—*their song*—that played softly between her heartbeats, a rhythm that had never stopped. Her breath caught in her throat as she took a step closer, the words she needed to say caught in the back of her throat.

The bard reached out, as if drawn by some invisible force. He took her hand, his fingers warm and certain, and in that touch, Lyra felt it. The connection. It was undeniable.

"I'm..." he started, his voice cracking slightly. "I'm not sure what's happening. But when you were singing, I—I felt like I knew you. Like... *we* knew each other."

Lyra looked at him, her mind racing, and the truth hit her all at once, sweeping over her like a crashing wave. He wasn't just a stranger. He wasn't just some random bard who had stumbled into her life. He was the *same*. The same soul. The same *love*. The same fate.

Tears welled in her eyes as she realized the truth. "Aris," she whispered, her voice breaking.

The bard blinked, his brow furrowing as though something stirred in his chest. "Aris?" he repeated, testing the name, as if it were unfamiliar yet familiar all at once.

Lyra nodded, her heart swelling with a mixture of joy and sorrow, knowing she could never undo the past. He had come back. Not in the way she had imagined, not in the way she had hoped, but here, now, in this moment, their song was still alive. He had been reborn, not as the man he once was, but as a new form—a new life. A new beginning.

The bard's expression shifted as if something within him recognized her, like a memory slowly surfacing from a long-forgotten dream. "I…" His voice trailed off, and for a moment, there was only silence between them. Then he spoke again, his voice barely a whisper, filled with wonder. "I remember you. *I remember.*"

The world around them seemed to still again. Time stretched. Lyra held her breath. In that instant, she saw him. She saw *Aris* in him—saw the same warmth in his eyes, the same love that had once bound them together. But this time, there was no fear of losing him. No sorrow at the price they had paid. The Loom had been restored, the world had been rewritten, but in this moment, Lyra understood: the past was never truly gone. It had just woven itself into a new thread.

The song that had once tied them together had never truly ended. It had merely been waiting, waiting for the right moment, waiting for them to find each other again.

She reached for him, her heart full, her soul resonating with the music they had created together. And this time, as their hands met once more, she didn't let go. This time, the bond between them was no longer fragile, no longer torn by the threads of fate. It was whole. Complete. It was *theirs*.

Together, they began to hum the first few notes of their song, the same melody that had once been lost in silence. But now, it wasn't just a memory. It was alive, filling the air around them, growing stronger with every breath they took, every note they sang. The world began to hum with it, as if the earth itself was alive with their song.

And as they stood there, together, Lyra knew—this time, their love would never be undone. Fate had woven them together once more, and no matter what came next, they would always find each other. Always.

The final note hung in the air, and as it faded, Lyra smiled through her tears. She had found him again. The song that had never been sung was finally complete.

And their fates—forever intertwined—would echo through time.